ADRIENNE RICH'S POETRY

TEXTS OF THE POEMS

THE POET ON HER WORK

REVIEWS AND CRITICISM

By Adrienne Rich

ADRIENNE RICH'S POETRY

TEXTS OF THE POEMS
THE POET ON HER WORK
REVIEWS AND CRITICISM

➤➤◀◀

Selected and Edited by

BARBARA CHARLESWORTH GELPI
ALBERT GELPI

STANFORD UNIVERSITY

➤➤ ◀◀

W · W · NORTON & COMPANY · INC · *New York*

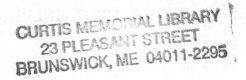

Contents

The Poet on Her Work

Criticism

Preface

Time and again after one of Adrienne Rich's readings on campuses around the country the audience crowds up to the stage for a closer glimpse of her, the chance of a word with her. Her poems generate the same kind of response in the classroom; students feel an excitement and engagement so unusual in reading poetry that it sometimes startles them, as both of us have found in teaching Adrienne Rich's work on different levels, from freshman to graduate students. The magnetism of her presence and of her work comes partly from the sense of a personality which has centered and freed itself in a way that very few of us have, and, more than that, of a personality which in the very process of self-discovery finds the language to describe the process, reaches us with a voice, and so helps us to reach ourselves. That voice speaks to those who lived through the bewildering sixties, but it speaks with equal force to the present generation of students. For all recognize with the same urgency the desire to be freed and centered, and all can find the difficulties of the process, the failures, tragedies, and sudden breakthroughs into new vision given clarity and scope in Rich's poetry. The person whom her poems move to define is a woman, herself, the poet, and so her work is of special importance for women. But men too can feel the power and depth of her language and find themselves refracted in its images.

To teach Rich's poetry, to write and talk about it, to discuss it with students, we have invariably found, is to have the sense of being at the focus of energies—and that makes for the happiest and most stimulating teaching and learning. This book was planned for use in a variety of courses: poetry courses, women's studies, freshman writing. The Introduction seeks to place Adrienne Rich, however sketchily, in the historical development of women's poetry during the last century. The first section contains a representative selection from all eight of Rich's published volumes. (Rich began dating her poems after the first two volumes, out of a deepening sense that poems arise from a particular point in the flow of time, and that poetry is inseparable from the process of living, changing, and developing; we have, therefore, followed her dating of poems here.)

The next section brings together commentary by the poet on her work and on the ideas and attitudes which provide a context for her work: a statement from the middle sixties about her changing notions of the sources and the function of poetry, which stands as a concise summary of contemporary poetics; autobiographical reflections on her own experience as a woman poet in the patriarchy; excerpts from the long review-essay which was in effect her public declaration as a radical feminist and which has become a widely influential document in the women's movement; and a series of informal, free-wheeling conversations, recorded for this book, about poetry, politics, and psychology, and how they intersect.

The third section offers a balanced selection from the already considerable body of criticism on Rich's poetry from different approaches and with differing evaluative judgments and conclusions. Then, since the poetry is having an ever-increasing impact on the ways in which women see and think about themselves, we have added to the previously published criticism two essays by women who are very much aware of the changes in women's consciousness and are themselves instrumental in helping to create new attitudes. We asked Wendy Martin, the editor of *Women's Studies,* who is now working on a book about American women writers, and Nancy Milford, Zelda Fitzgerald's biographer, at present writing a life of Edna St. Vincent Millay, to write pieces for publication here. Their essays are personal readings of Rich's work, each discussing from her own perspective how deeply the poems have registered, individually and collectively, on her sensibility.

At the end of the book there are: a Chronology of the poet's life and career; a Bibliography of her writings—the first complete listing, current as of publication; and a reference Index.

The editors wish to thank especially John Benedict, who conceived this project and suggested it to us; Josephine Guttadauro, who, in addition to typing much of the manuscript, reduced the taped conversations to a manageable transcript; and Adrienne Rich, who provided not only the material of this volume but, for us at least, much of the spirit as well.

BARBARA CHARLESWORTH GELPI
ALBERT GELPI

Introduction

Adrienne Rich would be a remarkable poet in any context, but in her work poetry by women comes more definitively and boldly into its own. She did not of course achieve this alone. Far from it; there were women before her—and not only women thinkers and artists—and there are contemporary women whose existence and situation make a decisive difference for her, and she would insist on remaining in that circle of women. But it is becoming increasingly clear that within the circle she stands with special presence as pioneer, witness, prophet: at once realist and dreamer. Although these archetypal roles carry strong masculine associations in the American mythology, her poetry, and the movement for which it is a center, may herald, testify to, and effect a shift in consciousness which could only end in a change in our social structures and, simultaneously, in our mythology.

It is not surprising to find Adrienne Rich drawn to both Walt Whitman and Emily Dickinson: Whitman projecting an ideal America beyond divisive polarities, including the sexual; Dickinson keeping a polar privacy in her bedroom under her father's roof and yet "having it out at last," as Adrienne Rich wrote of her, "on her own premises." From the beginning Rich's theme, personal and collective, has been woman in the patriarchy: her own identity, the identity of woman on man's established terms; and, more and more urgently, the possibility of identity on her own, on woman's own terms.

In a conversation in this book Adrienne Rich describes the writing of most women as having the quality of "banked fires." Like Dickinson, women poets until very recently have managed to have it out on something like their own premises only by denying or inhibiting one aspect of themselves or the other: on the one hand, exploring the risks of love and the convolutions of sensibility, at best with subtlety, at worst with sentimentality; or, on the other hand, suspiciously repressing or deflecting their emotional and sexual nature in the name of intellectual clarity and discursive crispness. Edna St. Vincent Millay, Elinor Wylie, and Sara Teasdale might be seen to fall principally into the first broad category; Marianne Moore, Elizabeth Bishop, and Louise Bogan principally into the second. Harder to place, H. D. is generally associated with Imagism, her intensities faceted in cool surfaces; but actually her best work, written during the Second World War and the Cold War, went far beyond Imagism. Nevertheless, although her imagination was responding in large part to the political and social upheavals of that period, her response was characteristically "womanly": she did not engage the political realities directly (as Pound did in *The Pisan Cantos*), but withdrew further and further inward to celebrate the psychological and mystical dimensions of woman's mysteries.

The breakthrough in women's poetry came as part of the radical political consciousness of the 1960's, and the questioning of social ideology and structures which the protest against the Indochina war engendered, and in the forefront were Denise Levertov and Adrienne Rich. In reviewing Robin Morgan's book of poems, *Monster,* Rich sketched out the evolution of women's poetry during the last century:

> The history of women poets has been a history of [the] partial internalization [of masculine thought and attitudes]. The last hundred years, besides giving us Emily Dickinson, Christina Rossetti, and the remarkable, obscure suicide, Charlotte Mew, also gave us a number of women poets marked by the depressive mood, their sense that to act was to court destruction. Vague sorrow, chaste ironic coolness, veiled whatever realities of sexual ambivalence, bitterness, frustration were experienced by such women as Louise Guiney, Sara Teasdale, Elinor Wylie and their lesser-known contemporaries. Edna Millay alone seems a precursor of what was to come, and only at times. Marianne Moore fled into a universe of forms; H. D. (Hilda Doolittle) to the more fertile religion of myth.
> But in the last decade and a half new possibilities opened up in American poetry. Psychoanalysis, increased verbal and sexual freedom, a more organic and open poetic mode such as Denise Levertov's and Carolyn Kizer's, combined to release women's poetry from the discreet, the melancholy, the sentimental, the merely ethereal. Most notably, Anne Sexton and Sylvia Plath, in their very different voices, began to speak of the quarrel with themselves—which was found to be also the quarrel with others. * * *
> In both Plath and [Diane] Wakoski a subjective, personal rage blazes forth, never before seen in women's poetry. If it is unnerving it is also cathartic, the blowtorch of language cleansing the rust and ticky-tacky and veneer from an entire consciousness. In Robin Morgan's *Monster* this same force is politicized, shared with other women, offered to them as a sounding board, a voice at the end of some hotline. Morgan writes not simply out of her personal intention to survive but out of a vision of the survival and transformation of all women.[1]

The distinction which Rich is making in the last paragraph explains why she and Morgan are feminist poets, and Plath and Wakowski are not. In Rich's development the private poet becomes a public

1. *The Washington Post Book World,* December 31, 1972, p. 3.

poet without sacrificing the complexity of subjective experience or the intensity of personal emotion. We can hear Dickinson's quandary breaking out, reaching into rhythms which reclaim, on women's terms, Whitman's prophetic call to a society of individuals.

THE EDITORS

Texts of the Poems

From *A Change of World*
(1951)

Storm Warnings

The glass has been falling all the afternoon,
And knowing better than the instrument
What winds are walking overhead, what zone
Of gray unrest is moving across the land,
I leave the book upon a pillowed chair
And walk from window to closed window, watching
Boughs strain against the sky

And think again, as often when the air
Moves inward toward a silent core of waiting,
How with a single purpose time has traveled
By secret currents of the undiscerned
Into this polar realm. Weather abroad
And weather in the heart alike come on
Regardless of prediction.

Between foreseeing and averting change
Lies all the mastery of elements
Which clocks and weatherglasses cannot alter.
Time in the hand is not control of time,
Nor shattered fragments of an instrument
A proof against the wind; the wind will rise,
We can only close the shutters.

I draw the curtains as the sky goes black
And set a match to candles sheathed in glass
Against the keyhole draught, the insistent whine
Of weather through the unsealed aperture.
This is our sole defense against the season;
These are the things that we have learned to do
Who live in troubled regions.

Aunt Jennifer's Tigers

Aunt Jennifer's tigers prance across a screen,
Bright topaz denizens of a world of green.
They do not fear the men beneath the tree;
They pace in sleek chivalric certainty.

Aunt Jennifer's fingers fluttering through her wool
Find even the ivory needle hard to pull.
The massive weight of Uncle's wedding band
Sits heavily upon Aunt Jennifer's hand.

When Aunt is dead, her terrified hands will lie
Still ringed with ordeals she was mastered by.
The tigers in the panel that she made
Will go on prancing, proud and unafraid.

Afterward

Now that your hopes are shamed, you stand
At last believing and resigned,
And none of us who touch your hand
Know how to give you back in kind
The words you flung when hopes were proud:
Being born to happiness
Above the asking of the crowd,
You would not take a finger less.
We who know limits now give room
To one who grows to fit her[1] doom.

The Uncle Speaks in
the Drawing Room

I have seen the mob of late
Standing sullen in the square,
Gazing with a sullen stare
At window, balcony, and gate.
Some have talked in bitter tones,
Some have held and fingered stones.

1. When the poem appeared in *A Change of World,* the phrase read "his doom." Amending the phrase in *Poems: Selected and New* the poet noted: "I have altered the [pronoun] not simply as a matter of fact but because [it alters], for me, the dimensions of the poem."

These are follies that subside.
Let us consider, none the less,
Certain frailties of glass
Which, it cannot be denied,
Lead in times like these to fear
For crystal vase and chandelier.

Not that missiles will be cast;
None as yet dare lift an arm.
But the scene recalls a storm
When our grandsire stood aghast
To see his antique ruby bowl
Shivered in a thunder-roll.

Let us only bear in mind
How these treasures handed down
From a calmer age passed on
Are in the keeping of our kind.
We stand between the dead glass-blowers
And murmurings of missile-throwers.

An Unsaid Word

She who has power to call her man
From that estranged intensity
Where his mind forages alone,
Yet keeps her peace and leaves him free,
And when his thoughts to her return
Stands where he left her, still his own,
Knows this the hardest thing to learn.

From *The Diamond Cutters and Other Poems*
(1955)

Pictures by Vuillard[1]

Now we remember all: the wild pear-tree,
The broken ribbons of the green-and-gold
Portfolio, with sketches from an old
Algerian campaign; the placid three
Women at coffee by the window, fates
Of nothing ominous, waiting for the ring
Of the postman's bell; we harbor everything—
The cores of fruit left on the luncheon plates.
We are led back where we have never been,
Midday where nothing's tragic, all's delayed
As it should have been for us as well—that shade
Of summer always, Neuilly[2] dappled green!

But we, the destined readers of Stendhal,[3]
In monstrous change such consolations find
As restless mockery sets before the mind
To deal with what must anger and appall.
Much of the time we scarcely think of sighing
For afternoons that found us born too late.
Our prudent envy rarely paces spying
Under those walls, that lilac-shadowed gate.
Yet at this moment, in our private view,
A breath of common peace, like memory,
Rustles the branches of the wild pear-tree—
Air that we should have known, and cannot know.

---

1. Edouard Vuillard (1868–1940), a post-Impressionist painter, noted for domestic scenes small in scale and intimate in effect.
2. A suburb northwest of the center of Paris.
3. Pen name of Henri Beyle (1783–1842), author of *The Red and the Black* and *The Charterhouse of Parma*, novels which view history and life ironically.

Love in the Museum

Now will you stand for me, in this cool light,
Infanta[4] reared in ancient etiquette,
A point-lace queen of manners. At your feet
The doll-like royal dog demurely set
Upon a chequered floor of black and white.

Or be a Louis' mistress, by Boucher,[5]
Lounging on cushions, silken feet asprawl
Upon a couch where casual cupids play
While on your arms and shoulders seems to fall
The tired extravagance of a sunset day.

Or let me think I pause beside a door
And see you in a bodice by Vermeer,[6]
Where light falls quartered on the polished floor
And rims the line of water tilting clear
Out of an earthen pitcher as you pour.

But art requires a distance: let me be
Always the connoisseur of your perfection.
Stay where the spaces of the gallery
Flow calm between your pose and my inspection,
Lest one imperfect gesture make demands
As troubling as the touch of human hands.

Ideal Landscape

We had to take the world as it was given:
The nursemaid sitting passive in the park
Was rarely by a changeling prince accosted.
The mornings happened similar and stark
In rooms of selfhood where we woke and lay
Watching today unfold like yesterday.

Our friends were not unearthly beautiful,
Nor spoke with tongues of gold; our lovers blundered
Now and again when most we sought perfection,

4. Diego Velasquez (1599–1660), court painter to Philip IV of Spain, painted many portraits of the royal family, among them several of the Infanta Maria Teresa and of the Infanta Margarita.
5. François Boucher (1703–1770) patronized by Mme. de la Pompadour, mistress of Louis XV.
6. Jan Vermeer (1632–1675), Dutch painter of domestic scenes.

Or hid in cupboards when the heavens thundered.
The human rose to haunt us everywhere,
Raw, flawed, and asking more than we could bear.

And always time was rushing like a tram
Through streets of a foreign city, streets we saw
Opening into great and sunny squares
We could not find again, no map could show—
Never those fountains tossed in that same light,
Those gilded trees, those statues green and white.

The Middle-aged

Their faces, safe as an interior
Of Holland tiles and Oriental carpet,
Where the fruit-bowl, always filled, stood in a light
Of placid afternoon—their voices' measure,
Their figures moving in the Sunday garden
To lay the tea outdoors or trim the borders,
Afflicted, haunted us. For to be young
Was always to live in other peoples' houses
Whose peace, if we sought it, had been made by others,
Was ours at second-hand and not for long.
The custom of the house, not ours, the sun
Fading the silver-blue Fortuny[7] curtains,
The reminiscence of a Christmas party
Of fourteen years ago—all memory,
Signs of possession and of being possessed,
We tasted, tense with envy. They were so kind,
Would have given us anything; the bowl of fruit
Was filled for us, there was a room upstairs
We must call ours: but twenty years of living
They could not give. Nor did they ever speak
Of the coarse stain on that polished balustrade,
The crack in the study window, or the letters
Locked in a drawer and the key destroyed.
All to be understood by us, returning
Late, in our own time—how that peace was made,
Upon what terms, with how much left unsaid.

7. With designs based on those of Moorish fourteenth-century ceramic tiles.

Living in Sin

She had thought the studio would keep itself;
no dust upon the furniture of love.
Half heresy, to wish the taps less vocal,
the panes relieved of grime. A plate of pears,
a piano with a Persian shawl, a cat
stalking the picturesque amusing mouse
had risen at his urging.
Not that at five each separate stair would writhe
under the milkman's tramp; that morning light
so coldly would delineate the scraps
of last night's cheese and three sepulchral bottles;
that on the kitchen shelf among the saucers
a pair of beetle-eyes would fix her own—
Envoy from some village in the moldings . . .
Meanwhile, he, with a yawn,
sounded a dozen notes upon the keyboard,
declared it out of tune, shrugged at the mirror,
rubbed at his beard, went out for cigarettes;
while she, jeered by the minor demons,
pulled back the sheets and made the bed and found
a towel to dust the table-top,
and let the coffee-pot boil over on the stove.
By evening she was back in love again,
though not so wholly but throughout the night
she woke sometimes to feel the daylight coming
like a relentless milkman up the stairs.

A Walk by the Charles[8]

Finality broods upon the things that pass:
Persuaded by this air, the trump of doom
Might hang unsounded while the autumn gloom
Darkens the leaf and smokes the river's glass.
For nothing so susceptible to death
But on this forenoon seems to hold its breath:
The silent single oarsmen on the stream
Are always young, are rowers in a dream.
The lovers underneath the chestnut tree,

8. A river flowing between Boston and Cambridge, Massachusetts.

Though love is over, stand bemused to see
The season falling where no fall could be.

You oarsmen, when you row beyond the bend,
Will see the river winding to its end.
Lovers that hold the chestnut burr in hand
Will speak at last of death, will understand,
Foot-deep amid the ruinage of the year,
What smell it is that stings the gathering air.

From our evasions we are brought at last,
From all our hopes of faithfulness, to cast
One look of recognition at the sky,
The unimportant leaves that flutter by.
Why else upon this bank are we so still?
What lends us anchor but the mutable?

O lovers, let the bridge of your two hands
Be broken, like the mirrored bridge that bends
And shivers on the surface of the stream.
Young oarsmen, who in timeless gesture seem
Continuous, united with the tide,
Leave off your bending to the oar, and glide
Past innocence, beyond these aging bricks
To where the Charles flows in to join the Styx.[9]

The Diamond Cutters

However legendary,
The stone is still a stone,
Though it had once resisted
The weight of Africa,
The hammer-blows of time
That wear to bits of rubble
The mountain and the pebble—
But not this coldest one.

Now, you intelligence
So late dredged up from dark
Upon whose smoky walls
Bison took fumbling form
Or flint was edged on flint—

9. In Green mythology, a river which flowed around the world of the dead.

Now, careful arriviste,[1]
Delineate at will
Incisions in the ice.

Be serious, because
The stone may have contempt
For too-familiar hands,
And because all you do
Loses or gains by this:
Respect the adversary,
Meet it with tools refined,
And thereby set your price.

Be hard of heart, because
The stone must leave your hand.
Although you liberate
Pure and expensive fires
Fit to enamor Shebas,[2]
Keep your desire apart.
Love only what you do,
And not what you have done.

Be proud, when you have set
The final spoke of flame
In that prismatic wheel,
And nothing's left this day
Except to see the sun
Shine on the false and the true,
And know that Africa
Will yield you more to do.

Letter from the Land of Sinners

I write you this out of another province
That you may never see:
Country of rivers, its topography
Mutable in detail, yet always one,
Blasted in certain places, here by glaciers,
There by the work of man.

1. Literally, one who has arrived; a social climber or upstart.
2. The Queen of Sheba, famed for her beauty and attractiveness, from a land located in the southwest corner of the Arabian peninsula. In the Old Testament, 1 Kings 10 describes her visit to the Israelite King Solomon.

The fishers by the water have no boast
Save of their freedom; here
A man may cast a dozen kinds of lure
And think his days rewarded if he sight
Now and again the prize, unnetted, flicking
Its prism-gleams of light.

The old lord lived secluded in his park
Until the hall was burned
Years ago, by his tenants; both have learned
Better since then, and now our children run
To greet him. Quail and hunter have forgotten
The echo of the gun.

I said there are blasted places: we have kept
Their nakedness intact—
No marble to commemorate an act
Superhuman or merely rash; we know
Why they are there and why the seed that falls there
Is certain not to grow.

We keep these places as we keep the time
Scarred on our recollection
When some we loved broke from us in defection,
Or we ourselves harried to death too soon
What we could least forgo. Our memories
Recur like the old moon.

But we have made another kind of peace,
And walk where boughs are green,
Forgiven by the selves that we have been,
And learning to forgive. Our apples taste
Sweeter this year; our gates are falling down,
And need not be replaced.

From *Snapshots of a Daughter-in-Law*
(1963)

The Knight

A knight rides into the noon,
and his helmet points to the sun,
and a thousand splintered suns
are the gaiety of his mail.
The soles of his feet glitter
and his palms flash in reply,
and under his crackling banner
he rides like a ship in sail.

A knight rides into the noon,
and only his eye is living,
a lump of bitter jelly
set in a metal mask,
betraying rags and tatters
that cling to the flesh beneath
and wear his nerves to ribbons
under the radiant casque.

Who will unhorse this rider
and free him from between
the walls of iron, the emblems
crushing his chest with their weight?
Will they defeat him gently,
or leave him hurled on the green,
his rags and wounds still hidden
under the great breastplate?

1957

Snapshots of a Daughter-in-Law

1.

You, once a belle in Shreveport,
with henna-colored hair, skin like a peachbud,
still have your dresses copied from that time,
and play a Chopin[1] prelude
called by Cortot:[2] *"Delicious recollections*
float like perfume through the memory."[3]

Your mind now, moldering like wedding-cake,
heavy with useless experience, rich
with suspicion, rumor, fantasy,
crumbling to pieces under the knife-edge
of mere fact. In the prime of your life.

Nervy, glowering, your daughter
wipes the teaspoons, grows another way.

2.

Banging the coffee-pot into the sink
she hears the angels chiding, and looks out
past the raked gardens to the sloppy sky.
Only a week since They said: *Have no patience.*

The next time it was: *Be insatiable.*
Then: *Save yourself; others you cannot save.*
Sometimes she's let the tapstream scald her arm,
a match burn to her thumbnail,

or held her hand above the kettle's snout
right in the woolly steam. They are probably angels,
since nothing hurts her anymore, except
each morning's grit blowing into her eyes.

3.

A thinking woman sleeps with monsters.
The beak that grips her, she becomes. And Nature,
that sprung-lidded, still commodious

---

1. Frederic François Chopin (1810–1849): Polish composer and pianist who settled in Paris in 1831.
2. Alfred Cortot (1877–1962): famous French pianist.

3. Cortot's notation for Prelude #7, Andantino, A Major, in the prefatory remarks of his *Chopin: 24 Preludes* (Paris, 1930).

steamer-trunk of *tempora* and *mores*[4]
gets stuffed with it all: the mildewed orange-flowers,
the female pills,[5] the terrible breasts
of Boadicea[6] beneath flat foxes' heads and orchids.

Two handsome women, gripped in argument,
each proud, acute, subtle, I hear scream
across the cut glass and majolica
like Furies[7] cornered from their prey:
The argument *ad feminam*,[8] all the old knives
that have rusted in my back, I drive in yours,
ma semblable, ma soeur![9]

4.

Knowing themselves too well in one another:
their gifts no pure fruition, but a thorn,
the prick filed sharp against a hint of scorn . . .
Reading while waiting
for the iron to heat,
writing, *My Life had stood—a Loaded Gun—*[1]
in that Amherst[2] pantry while the jellies boil and scum,
or, more often,
iron-eyed and beaked and purposed as a bird,
dusting everything on the whatnot every day of life.

5.

Dulce ridens, dulce loquens,[3]
she shaves her legs until they gleam
like petrified mammoth-tusk.

---

4. Literally, "times and customs," alluding perhaps to Cicero's phrase "O Tempora! O Mores!" in *Pro Rege Deiotaro,* II. 31 ("Alas! for the degeneracy of our times and the low standard of our morals!").
5. Remedies for menstrual pain.
6. British queen in the time of the Emperor Nero who led her people in a large though finally unsuccessful revolt against Roman rule.
7. Greek goddesses of vengeance.
8. Feminine version of the phrase "ad hominem," referring to an argument which appeals to personal interests, prejudices, or emotions rather than to reason or justice.

9. The last line of the poem "Au Lecteur" by Charles Baudelaire addresses "Hypocrite lecteur!—mon semblable,—mon frère!": "Hypocrite reader, like me, my brother"—not, as here, "my sister."
1. Emily Dickinson, *Complete Poems,* ed. T. H. Johnson, 1960, page 369 [*Rich's note*]. Poem 754 in the Johnson edition: II, 574 in the variorum *Poems* (Harvard University Press, 1955).
2. The Massachusetts town in which Emily Dickinson lived (1830–1886).
3. Latin for "sweetly laughing, sweetly speaking." Horace (Quintus Horatius Flaccus), Ode XIX, "Integer vitae," ll. 23–24.

6.

When to her lute Corinna sings[4]
neither words nor music are her own;
only the long hair dipping
over her cheek, only the song
of silk against her knees
and these
adjusted in reflections of an eye.

Poised, trembling and unsatisfied, before
an unlocked door, that cage of cages,
tell us, you bird, you tragical machine—
is this *fertilisante douleur?*[5] Pinned down
by love, for you the only natural action,
are you edged more keen
to prise the secrets of the vault? has Nature shown
her household books to you, daughter-in-law,
that her sons never saw?

7.

*"To have in this uncertain world some stay
which cannot be undermined, is
of the utmost consequence."*[6]
                            Thus wrote
a woman, partly brave and partly good,
who fought with what she partly understood.
Few men about her would or could do more,
hence she was labeled harpy, shrew and whore.

8.

"You all die at fifteen," said Diderot,[7]
and turn part legend, part convention.
Still, eyes inaccurately dream
behind closed windows blankening with steam.
Deliciously, all that we might have been,
all that we were—fire, tears,
wit, taste, martyred ambition—

---

4. First line of a poem by Thomas Campion (1567–1620).
5. French for "fertilizing or life-giving sorrow."
6. From Mary Wollstonecraft, *Thoughts on the Education of Daughters,* London, 1787 [*Rich's note*]. This sentence appears on page 34.

7. Denis Diderot (1713–1784): French philosopher, encyclopedist, playwright, and critic. "You all die at fifteen": "Vous mourez toutes a quinze ans," from the *Lettres à Sophie Volland,* quoted by Simone de Beauvoir in *Le Deuxième Sexe,* Vol. II, pp. 123–24 [*Rich's note*].

stirs like the memory of refused adultery
the drained and flagging bosom of our middle years.

9.

*Not that it is done well, but
that it is done at all?*[8] Yes, think
of the odds! or shrug them off forever.
This luxury of the precocious child,
Time's precious chronic invalid,—
would we, darlings, resign it if we could?
Our blight has been our sinecure:
mere talent was enough for us—
glitter in fragments and rough drafts.

Sigh no more, ladies.
                              Time is male
and in his cups drinks to the fair.
Bemused by gallantry, we hear
our mediocrities over-praised,
indolence read as abnegation,
slattern thought styled intuition,
every lapse forgiven, our crime
only to cast too bold a shadow
or smash the mold straight off.

For that, solitary confinement,
tear gas, attrition shelling.
Few applicants for that honor.

10.

                              Well,
she's long about her coming, who must be
more merciless to herself than history.
Her mind full to the wind, I see her plunge
breasted and glancing through the currents,
taking the light upon her
at least as beautiful as any boy

---

8. An allusion to Samuel Johnson's remark to Boswell: "Sir, a woman's preaching is like a dog's walking on his hinder legs. It is not done well; but you are surprised to find it done at all" (July 31, 1763, *Boswell's Life of Johnson*, ed. George Birkbeck Hill [Oxford, 1934], I, 463).

or helicopter,[9]
            poised, still coming,
her fine blades making the air wince

but her cargo
no promise then:
delivered
palpable
ours.

1958–1960

Antinoüs:[1] The Diaries

Autumn torture. The old signs
smeared on the pavement, sopping leaves
rubbed into the landscape as unguent on a bruise,
brought indoors, even, as they bring flowers, enormous,
with the colors of the body's secret parts.
All this. And then, evenings, needing to be out,
walking fast, fighting the fire
that must die, light that sets my teeth on edge with joy,
till on the black embankment
I'm a cart stopped in the ruts of time.

Then at some house the rumor of truth and beauty
saturates a room like lilac-water
in the steam of a bath, fires snap, heads are high,
gold hair at napes of necks, gold in glasses,
gold in the throat, poetry of furs and manners.
Why do I shiver then? Haven't I seen,
over and over, before the end of an evening,
the three opened coffins carried in and left in a corner?
Haven't I watched as somebody cracked his shin
on one of them, winced and hopped and limped

9. "She comes down from the remoteness of ages, from Thebes, from Crete, from Chichén-Itzá; and she is also the totem set deep in the African jungle; she is a helicopter and she is a bird; and there is this, the greatest wonder of all: under her tinted hair the forest murmur becomes a thought, and words issue from her breasts" (Simone de Beauvoir, *The Sec-*

ond Sex, trans. H. M. Parshley [New York, 1953], p. 729). (A translation of the passage from *Le Deuxième Sexe,* Vol. II, p. 574, cited in French by Rich.)
1. A beautiful youth, favorite boy of the Emperor Hadrian, who drowned in the Nile, perhaps a suicide, in A.D. 130. [I let the young man speak for me —*Rich's note.*]

laughing to lay his hand on a beautiful arm
striated with hairs of gold, like an almond-shell?

The old, needless story. For if I'm here
it is by choice and when at last
I smell my own rising nausea, feel the air
tighten around my stomach like a surgical bandage,
I can't pretend surprise. What is it I so miscarry?
If what I spew on the tiles at last,
helpless, disgraced, alone,
is in part what I've swallowed from glasses, eyes,
motions of hands, opening and closing mouths,
isn't it also dead gobbets of myself,
abortive, murdered, or never willed?

1959

The Afterwake

Nursing your nerves
to rest, I've roused my own; well,
now for a few bad hours!
Sleep sees you behind closed doors.
Alone, I slump in his front parlor.
You're safe inside. Good. But I'm
like a midwife who at dawn
has all in order: bloodstains
washed up, teapot on the stove,
and starts her five miles home
walking, the birthyell still
exploding in her head.

Yes, I'm with her now: here's
the streaked, livid road
edged with shut houses
breathing night out and in.
Legs tight with fatigue,
we move under morning's coal-blue star,
colossal as this load
of unexpired purpose, which drains
slowly, till scissors of cockcrow snip the air.

1961

A Marriage in the 'Sixties

As solid-seeming as antiquity,
you frown above
the *New York Sunday Times*
where Castro,[2] like a walk-on out of *Carmen*,[3]
mutters into a bearded henchman's ear.

They say the second's getting shorter—
I knew it in my bones—
and pieces of the universe are missing.
I feel the gears of this late afternoon
slip, cog by cog, even as I read.
"I'm old," we both complain,
half-laughing, oftener now.

Time serves you well. That face—
part Roman emperor, part Raimu[4]—
nothing this side of Absence can undo.
Bliss, revulsion, your rare angers can
only carry through what's well begun.

When
I read your letters long ago
in that half-defunct
hotel in Magdalen Street
every word primed my nerves.
A geographical misery
composed of oceans, fogbound planes
and misdelivered cablegrams
lay round me, a Nova Zembla[5]
only your live breath could unfreeze.
Today we stalk
in the raging desert of our thought
whose single drop of mercy is
each knows the other there.
Two strangers, thrust for life upon a rock,
may have at last the perfect hour of talk
that language aches for; still—
two minds, two messages.

2. Fidel Castro (1927–   ), Cuban leader who on January 1, 1959, overthrew the regime of General Fulgencio Batista in a Marxist revolution.
3. An opera (1875) by George Bizet (1838–1875) about a romance between a Spanish soldier and a gypsy woman.
4. Pseudonym of Jules Muraire (1883–1946), French character actor and comedian with a music-hall background.
5. An Arctic land off the coast of Russia.

Your brows knit into flourishes. Some piece
of mere time has you tangled there.
Some mote of history has flown into your eye.
Will nothing ever be the same,
even our quarrels take a different key,
our dreams exhume new metaphors?
The world breathes underneath our bed.
Don't look. We're at each other's mercy too.

Dear fellow-particle, electric dust
I'm blown with—ancestor
to what euphoric cluster—
see how particularity dissolves
in all that hints of chaos. Let one finger
hover toward you from There
and see this furious grain
suspend its dance to hang
beside you like your twin.

1961

The Roofwalker

—for Denise Levertov

Over the half-finished houses
night comes. The builders
stand on the roof. It is
quiet after the hammers,
the pulleys hang slack.
Giants, the roofwalkers,
on a listing deck, the wave
of darkness about to break
on their heads. The sky
is a torn sail where figures
pass magnified, shadows
on a burning deck.

I feel like them up there:
exposed, larger than life,
and due to break my neck.

Was it worth while to lay—
with infinite exertion—

a roof I can't live under?
—All those blueprints,
closings of gaps,
measurings, calculations?
A life I didn't choose
chose me: even
my tools are the wrong ones
for what I have to do.
I'm naked, ignorant,
a naked man fleeing
across the roofs
who could with a shade of difference
be sitting in the lamplight
against the cream wallpaper
reading—not with indifference—
about a naked man
fleeing across the roofs.

1961

Ghost of a Chance

You see a man
trying to think.

You want to say
to everything:
Keep off! Give him room!
But you only watch,
terrified
the old consolations
will get him at last
like a fish
half-dead from flopping
and almost crawling
across the shingle,
almost breathing
the raw, agonizing
air
till a wave
pulls it back blind into the triumphant
sea.

1962

Prospective Immigrants
Please Note

Either you will
go through this door
or you will not go through.

If you go through
there is always the risk
of remembering your name.

Things look at you doubly
and you must look back
and let them happen.

If you do not go through
it is possible
to live worthily

to maintain your attitudes
to hold your position
to die bravely

but much will blind you,
much will evade you,
at what cost who knows?

The door itself
makes no promises.
It is only a door.

1962

From *Necessities of Life*
(1966)

Necessities of Life[1]

Piece by piece I seem
to re-enter the world: I first began

a small, fixed dot, still see
that old myself, a dark-blue thumbtack

pushed into the scene,
a hard little head protruding

from the pointillist's   buzz and bloom.
After a time the dot

begins to ooze. Certain heats
melt it.
          Now I was hurriedly

blurring into ranges
of burnt red, burning green,

whole biographies swam up and
swallowed me like Jonah.[3]

Jonah! I was Wittgenstein,[4]
Mary Wollstonecraft,[5] the soul

of Louis Jouvet,[6] dead
in a blown-up photograph.

1. Entitled "Thirty-Three" when the poem first appeared in *The Paris Review* (Winter–Spring 1964).
2. Pointillism is a post-impressionist school of painting exemplified by Georges Seurat and his followers. They reduced color to its constituent shades and painted in dots of those shades, to be blended by the viewer's eye into the appropriate colors.
3. Old Testament prophet who was swallowed by a great fish and released after three days (Jonah 1:17).
4. Ludwig Wittgenstein (1889–1957), a philosopher especially important for his work in linguistic analysis and semantics.
5. Mary Wollstonecraft (1759–1797), English feminist, author of *A Vindication of the Rights of Woman*.
6. Louis Jouvet (1887–1957), French director, actor, designer and technician.

Till, wolfed almost to shreds,
I learned to make myself

unappetizing. Scaly as a dry bulb
thrown into a cellar
I used myself, let nothing use me.
Like being on a private dole,

sometimes more like kneading bricks in Egypt.[7]
What life was there, was mine,

now and again to lay
one hand on a warm brick

and touch the sun's ghost
with economical joy,

now and again to name
over the bare necessities.

So much for those days. Soon
practice may make me middling-perfect, I'll

dare inhabit the world
trenchant in motion as an eel, solid

as a cabbage-head. I have invitations:
a curl of mist steams upward

from a field, visible as my breath,
houses along a road stand waiting

like old women knitting, breathless
to tell their tales.

1962

In the Woods

"Difficult ordinary happiness,"[8]
no one nowadays believes in you.

---

7. The Israelites, when captive in Egypt, were set by the Pharaoh to making bricks for building his cities (Exodus 1:14).

8. The line is borrowed, translated from the Dutch poet J. C. Bloem [*Rich's note*].

I shift, full-length on the blanket,
to fix the sun precisely

behind the pine-tree's crest
so light spreads through the needles
alive as water just
where a snake has surfaced,

unreal as water in green crystal.
Bad news is always arriving.
"We're hiders, hiding from something bad,"[9]
sings the little boy.

Writing these words in the woods,
I feel like a traitor to my friends,
even to my enemies.
The common lot's to die

a stranger's death and lie
rouged in the coffin, in a dress
chosen by the funeral director.
Perhaps that's why we never

see clocks on public buildings any more.
A fact no architect will mention.
We're hiders, hiding from something bad
most of the time.

Yet, and outrageously, something good
finds us, found me this morning
lying on a dusty blanket
among the burnt-out Indian pipes

and bursting-open lady's-slippers.
My soul, my helicopter, whirred
distantly, by habit, over
the old pond with the half-drowned boat

toward which it always veers
for consolation: ego's Arcady:[1]
leaving the body stuck
like a leaf against a screen.—

9. Sung by the poet's son David at play.
1. An allusion to the phrase "et in Arcadia ego" ("and I in Arcadia"). Bartolomeo Schidoni (1560–1616) wrote on a painting, "Et in Arcadia vixi." ("And I lived in Arcadia.") The painters Guercino, Poussin, and Reynolds later put the phrase "Et in Arcadia ego" on paintings.

Happiness! how many times
I've stranded on that word,
at the edge of that pond; seen
as if through tears, the dragon-fly—

only to find it all
going differently for once
this time: my soul wheeled back
and burst into my body.

Found! Ready or not.
If I move now, the sun
naked between the trees
will melt me as I lie.

1963

The Trees

The trees inside are moving out into the forest,
the forest that was empty all these days
where no bird could sit
no insect hide
no sun bury its feet in shadow
the forest that was empty all these nights
will be full of trees by morning.

All night the roots work
to disengage themselves from the cracks
in the veranda floor.
The leaves strain toward the glass
small twigs stiff with exertion
long-cramped boughs shuffling under the roof
like newly discharged patients
half-dazed, moving
to the clinic doors.

I sit inside, doors open to the veranda
writing long letters
in which I scarcely mention the departure
of the forest from the house.
The night is fresh, the whole moon shines
in a sky still open

the smell of leaves and lichen
still reaches like a voice into the rooms.
My head is full of whispers
which tomorrow will be silent.

Listen. The glass is breaking.
The trees are stumbling forward
into the night. Winds rush to meet them.
The moon is broken like a mirror,
its pieces flash now in the crown
of the tallest oak.

1963

Like This Together

—for A.H.C.

1.

Wind rocks the car.
We sit parked by the river,
silence between our teeth.
Birds scatter across islands
of broken ice. Another time
I'd have said: "Canada geese,"
knowing you love them.
A year, ten years from now
I'll remember this—
this sitting like drugged birds
in a glass case—
not why, only that we
were here like this together.

2.

They're tearing down, tearing up
this city, block by block.
Rooms cut in half
hang like flayed carcasses,
their old roses in rags,
famous streets have forgotten
where they were going. Only
a fact could be so dreamlike.

They're tearing down the houses
we met and lived in,
soon our two bodies will be all
left standing from that era.

3.

We have, as they say,
certain things in common.
I mean: a view
from a bathroom window
over slate to stiff pigeons
huddled every morning; the way
water tastes from our tap,
which you marvel at, letting
it splash into the glass.
Because of you I notice
the taste of water,
a luxury I might
otherwise have missed.

4.

Our words misunderstand us.
Sometimes at night
you are my mother:
old detailed griefs
twitch at my dreams, and I
crawl against you, fighting
for shelter, making you
my cave. Sometimes
you're the wave of birth
that drowns me in my first
nightmare. I suck the air.
Miscarried knowledge twists us
like hot sheets thrown askew.

5.

Dead winter doesn't die,
it wears away, a piece of carrion
picked clean at last,
rained away or burnt dry.
Our desiring does this,
make no mistake, I'm speaking
of fact: through mere indifference

we could prevent it.
Only our fierce attention
gets hyacinths out of those
hard cerebral lumps,
unwraps the wet buds down
the whole length of a stem.[2]

1963

After Dark[3]

1.

You are falling asleep and I sit looking at you
old tree of life
old man whose death I wanted
I can't stir you up now.

Faintly a phonograph needle
whirs round in the last groove
eating my heart to dust.
That terrible record! how it played

down years, wherever I was
in foreign languages even
over and over, *I know you better*
than you know yourself   I know

you better than you know
yourself   I know
you   until, self-maimed,
I limped off, torn at the roots,

stopped singing a whole year,
got a new body, new breath,
got children, croaked for words,
forgot to listen

2. When this poem first appeared in
Poetry (April–May 1965) it had the fol-
lowing sixth and concluding stanza:

A severed hand
keeps tingling, air still suffers
beyond the stump. But new
life? How do we bear it
(or you, huge tree)
when fresh flames start spurting
out through our old sealed skins,

nerve-endings ours and not yet ours?
Susceptibilities we still
can't use, sucking
blind power from our roots—
what else to do but
hold fast to the
one thing we know,
grip earth and let burn.

3. The poem is an elegy for the poet's
father, Dr. Arnold Rich.

or read your *mene tekel*[4] fading on the wall,
woke up one morning
and knew myself your daughter.
Blood is a sacred poison.

Now, unasked, you give ground.
We only want to stifle
what's stifling us already.
Alive now, root to crown, I'd give

—oh,—something—not to know
our struggles now are ended.
I seem to hold you, cupped
in my hands, and disappearing.

When your memory fails—
no more to scourge my inconsistencies—
the sashcords of the world fly loose.
A window crashes

suddenly down. I go to the woodbox
and take a stick of kindling
to prop the sash again.
I grow protective toward the world.

2.

Now let's away from prison[5]—
Underground seizures!
I used to huddle in the grave
I'd dug for you and bite
my tongue for fear it would babble
—*Darling*—
I thought they'd find me there
someday, sitting upright, shrunken,

my hair like roots and in my lap
a mess of broken pottery—
wasted libation—
and you embalmed beside me.

4. The words which appeared on the walls of Belshazzar's feasting room and which the prophet Daniel interpreted correctly as signifying the king's downfall (Daniel 5).

5. Lear says to his faithful daughter Cordelia, captured and near death: "Come, let's away to prison" (Shakespeare, *King Lear*, V.iii.8).

No, let's away. Even now
there's a walk between doomed elms
(whose like we shall not see much longer)
and something—grass and water—

an old dream-photograph.
I'll sit with you there and tease you
for wisdom, if you like,
waiting till the blunt barge

bumps along the shore.
Poppies burn in the twilight
like smudge pots.
I think you hardly see me

but—this is the dream now—
your fears blow out,
off, over the water.
At the last, your hand feels steady.

1964

"I Am in Danger—Sir—"[6]

"Half-cracked"[7] to Higginson, living,
afterward famous in garbled versions,
your hoard of dazzling scraps a battlefield,
now your old snood

mothballed at Harvard[8]
and you in your variorum monument[9]
equivocal to the end—
who are you?

---

6. A sentence in a letter from Emily Dickinson to Thomas Wentworth Higginson (1823–1911), a literary critic with whom she opened correspondence in 1862 and to whom she sent some of her poems (*The Letters of Emily Dickinson*, ed. Thomas H. Johnson and Theodora Ward, 3 vols. [Cambridge, Mass., 1958], II, 409). She writes: "You think my gait 'spasmodic'—I am in danger—Sir—You think me 'uncontrolled'—I have no Tribunal."

7. Higginson in a letter described Emily Dickinson as "my partially cracked poetess at Amherst" (Jay Leyda, ed., *The Years and Hours of Emily Dickinson* [New Haven, 1960], II, 263.
8. The Houghton Rare Books Library at Harvard University has a collection of Emily Dickinson manuscripts and memorabilia.
9. *The Poems of Emily Dickinson*, ed. Thomas H. Johnson, 3 vols. (Cambridge, Mass., 1955).

Gardening the day-lily,
wiping the wine-glass stems,
your thought pulsed on behind
a forehead battered paper-thin,

you, woman, masculine
in single-mindedness,
for whom the word was more
than a symptom—

a condition of being.
Till the air buzzing with spoiled language
sang in your ears
of Perjury

and in your half-cracked way you chose
silence for entertainment,
chose to have it out at last
on your own premises.

1964

Mourning Picture

*(The picture was painted by Edwin Romanzo Elmer (1850–1923) as
a memorial to his daughter Effie. In the poem, it is the dead girl who
speaks.)*

They have carried the mahogany chair and the cane rocker
out under the lilac bush,
and my father and mother darkly sit there, in black clothes.
Our clapboard house stands fast on its hill,
my doll lies in her wicker pram
gazing at western Massachusetts.
This was our world.
I could remake each shaft of grass
feeling its rasp on my fingers,
draw out the map of every lilac leaf
or the net of veins on my father's
grief-tranced hand.

Out of my head, half-bursting,
still filling, the dream condenses—

shadows, crystals, ceilings, meadows, globes of dew.
Under the dull green of the lilacs, out in the light
carving each spoke of the pram, the turned porch-pillars,
under high early-summer clouds,
I am Effie, visible and invisible,
remembering and remembered.

They will move from the house,
give the toys and pets away.
Mute and rigid with loss my mother
will ride the train to Baptist Corner,
the silk-spool will run bare.
I tell you, the thread that bound us lies
faint as a web in the dew.
Should I make you, world, again,
could I give back the leaf its skeleton, the air
its early-summer cloud, the house
its noonday presence, shadowless,
and leave *this* out? I am Effie, you were my dream.

1965

Not Like That

It's so pure in the cemetery.
The children love to play up here.
It's a little town, a game of blocks,
a village packed in a box,
a pre-war German toy.
The turf is a bedroom carpet:
heal-all, strawberry flower
and hillocks of moss.
To come and sit here forever,
a cup of tea on one's lap
and one's eyes closed lightly, lightly,
perfectly still
in a nineteenth-century sleep!
it seems so normal to die.

Nobody sleeps here, children.
The little beds of white wrought iron
and the tall, kind, faceless nurse
are somewhere else, in a hospital
or the dreams of prisoners of war.

The drawers of this trunk are empty,
not even a snapshot
curls in a corner.

In Pullmans[1] of childhood we lay
enthralled behind dark-green curtains,
and a little lamp burned blue
all night, for us. The day
was a dream too, even the oatmeal
under its silver lid, dream-cereal
spooned out in forests of spruce
skirting the green-black gorges,
thick woods of sleep, half prickle,
half lakes of fern.
To stay here forever
is not like that, nor even
simply to lie quite still,
the warm trickle of dream
staining the thick quiet.
The drawers of this trunk are empty.
They are all out of sleep up here.

Focus

—for Bert Dreyfus

Obscurity has its tale to tell.
Like the figure on the studio-bed in the corner,

out of range, smoking, watching and waiting.
Sun pours through the skylight onto the worktable

making of a jar of pencils, a typewriter keyboard
more than they were. Veridical[2] light . . .

Earth budges. Now an empty coffee-cup,
a whetstone, a handkerchief, take on

their sacramental clarity, fixed by the wand
of light as the thinker thinks to fix them in the mind.

---

1. A railroad parlor car or sleeping car.   2. Truth-telling.

O secret in the core of the whetstone, in the five
pencils splayed out like fingers of a hand!

The mind's passion is all for singling out.
Obscurity has another tale to tell.

1965

Face to Face

Never to be lonely like that—
the Early American figure on the beach
in black coat and knee-breeches
scanning the didactic storm in privacy,

never to hear the prairie wolves
in their lunar hilarity
circling one's little all, one's claim
to be Law and Prophets

for all that lawlessness,
never to whet the appetite
weeks early, for a face, a hand
longed-for and dreaded—

How people used to meet!
starved, intense, the old
Christmas gifts saved up till spring,
and the old plain words,

and each with his God-given secret,
spelled out through months of snow and silence,
burning under the bleached scalp; behind dry lips
a loaded gun.[3]

1965

3. See *The Poems of Emily Dickinson,* ed. Thomas H. Johnson (Cambridge, Mass., 1955), II, 574. Poem 754 begins: "My Life—had stood a Loaded Gun—."

From *Leaflets*
(1969)

Orion[1]

Far back when I went zig-zagging
through tamarack pastures
you were my genius, you
my cast-iron Viking, my helmed
lion-heart king in prison.[2]
Years later now you're young

my fierce half-brother, staring
down from that simplified west
your breast open, your belt dragged down
by an oldfashioned thing, a sword
the last bravado you won't give over
though it weighs you down as you stride

and the stars in it are dim
and maybe have stopped burning.
But you burn, and I know it;
as I throw back my head to take you in
an old transfusion happens again:
divine astronomy is nothing to it.

Indoors I bruise and blunder,
break faith, leave ill enough
alone, a dead child born in the dark.
Night cracks up over the chimney,
pieces of time, frozen geodes[3]
come showering down in the grate.

1. A constellation which dominates the
winter in the northern hemisphere, named
for a mythical hunter of gigantic size and
great beauty. The belt and sword are
stars in the constellation.
2. Richard the Lion Heart of England

(1157–1199) was captured by Leopold
of Austria and imprisoned. According to
legend, his faithful minstrel Blondel dis-
covered his whereabouts.
3. A small, hollow, usually spheroidal
rock with crystals lining the inside wall.

A man reaches behind my eyes
and finds them empty
a woman's head turns away
from my head in the mirror
children are dying my death
and eating crumbs of my life.

Pity is not your forte.
Calmly you ache up there
pinned aloft in your crow's nest,
my speechless pirate!
You take it all for granted
and when I look you back

it's with a starlike eye
shooting its cold and egotistical spear
where it can do least damage.
Breathe deep! No hurt, no pardon
out here in the cold with you
you with your back to the wall.[4]

1965

In the Evening

Three hours chain-smoking words
and you move on. We stand in the porch,
two archaic figures: a woman and a man.

The old masters, the old sources,
haven't a clue what we're about,
shivering here in the half-dark 'sixties.

Our minds hover in a famous impasse
and cling together. Your hand
grips mine like a railing on an icy night.

---

4. One or two phrases suggested by Gottfried Benn's essay "Artists and Old Age" in *Primal Vision,* edited by E. B. Ashton, New Directions [*Rich's note*]. Benn writes this advice to the modern artist: "Don't lose sight of the cold and egotistical element in your mission. . . . With your back to the wall, care-worn and weary, in the gray light of the void, read Job and Jeremiah and keep going" (pp. 206–7).

The wall of the house is bleeding. Firethorn![5]
The moon, cracked every-which-way,
pushes steadily on.

1966

The Demon Lover

Fatigue, regrets. The lights
go out in the parking lot
two by two. Snow blindness
settles over the suburb.
Desire. Desire. The nebula
opens in space, unseen,
your heart utters its great beats
in solitude. A new
era is coming in.
Gauche as we are, it seems
we have to play our part.

A plaid dress, silk scarf,
and eyes that go on stinging.
Woman, stand off. The air
glistens like silk.
She's gone. In her place stands
a schoolgirl, morning light,
the half-grown bones
of innocence. Is she
your daughter or your muse,
this tree of blondness
grown up in a field of thorns?

Something piercing and marred.
Take note. Look back. When quick
the whole northeast went black
and prisoners howled and children
ran through the night with candles,
who stood off motionless
side by side while the moon swam up

5. A thorny shrub of the genus pyra-
cantha.
6. A phrase which Samuel Taylor Cole-
ridge uses in the poem "Kubla Khan."
7. On November 9, 1965, eight north-
eastern states and the province of On-
tario were entirely without electricity be-
cause of a massive power failure, for
periods ranging from thirty minutes in
some areas to thirteen hours in others.

over the drowned houses?
Who neither touched nor spoke?
whose nape, whose finger-ends
nervelessly lied the hours away?

A voice presses at me.
If I give in it won't
be like the girl the bull rode,
all Rubens flesh and happy moans.[8]
But to be wrestled like a boy
with tongue, hips, knees, nerves, brain . . .
with language?
He doesn't know. He's watching
breasts under a striped blouse,
his bull's head down. The old
wine pours again through my veins.

Goodnight. then. 'Night. Again
we turn our backs and weary
weary we let down.
Things take us hard, no question.
*How do you make it, all the way
from here to morning?* I touch
you, made of such nerve
and flare and pride and swallowed tears.
Go home. Come to bed. The skies
look in at us, stern.
And this is an old story.

I dreamed about the war.
We were all sitting at table
in a kitchen in Chicago.
The radio had just screamed
that Illinois was the target.
No one felt like leaving,
we sat by the open window
and talked in the sunset.
I'll tell you that joke tomorrow,
you said with your saddest smile,
if I can remember.

The end is just a straw,
a feather furling slowly down,

8. Europa, whom Zeus, taking the form of a bull, seduced and carried over to Crete. Peter Paul Rubens (1577–1640) painted the *The Rape of Europa*.

floating to light by chance, a breath
on the long-loaded scales.
Posterity trembles like a leaf
and we go on making heirs and heirlooms.
The world, we have to make it,
my coexistent friend[9] said, leaning
back in his cell.
Siberia vastly hulks
behind him, which he did not make.

Oh futile tenderness
of touch in a world like this!
how much longer, dear child,
do you think sex will matter?
There might have been a wedding
that never was:
two creatures sprung free
from castiron covenants.
Instead our hands and minds
erotically waver . . .
Lightness is unavailing.

Catalpas[1] wave and spill
their dull strings across this murk of spring.
I ache, brilliantly.
Only where there is language is there world.
In the harp of my hair, compose me
a song. Death's in the air,
we all know that. Still, for an hour,
I'd like to be gay. How could a gay song go?
Why that's your secret, and it shall be mine.
We are our words, and black and bruised and blue.
Under our skins, we're laughing.

In triste veritas?[2]
Take hold, sweet hands, come on . . .
Broken!
When you falter, all eludes.
This is a seasick way,
this almost/never touching, this
drawing-off, this to-and-fro.

---

9. "Peaceful co-existence" is a phrase used to describe the détente between the U.S.S.R. and the U.S.A. after the Cold War of the late forties and fifties.
1. The catalpa is a tree with large leaves, showy clusters of whitish flowers, and long, slender pods.
2. Literally, "in sorrow, truth," playing upon the phrase "in vino veritas": "in wine (drunkenness), truth."

Subtlety stalks in your eyes,
your tongue knows what it knows.
I want your secrets—I *will* have them out.
Seasick, I drop into the sea.

1966

The Key

Through a drain grating, something
    glitters and falters,
        glitters again. A scrap of foil,

a coin, a signal, a message
    from the indistinct
        piercing my indistinctness?

How long I have gone round
    and round, spiritless with foreknown defeat,
        in search of that glitter?

Hours, years maybe. The cry of metal
    on asphalt, on iron, the sudden
        ching of a precious loss,

the clear statement
    of something missing. Over and over
        it stops me in my tracks

like a falling star, only
    this is not the universe's loss
        it is mine. If I were only colder,

nearer death, nearer birth, I might let go
    whatever's so bent on staying lost.
        Why not leave the house

locked, to collapse inward among its weeds,
    the letters to darken and flake
        in the drawer, the car

to grow skeletal, aflame with rust
    in the moonlit lot, and walk
        ever after?

O God I am not spiritless,
    but a spirit can be stunned,
        a battery felt going dead

before the light flickers,
and I've covered this ground too often
with this yellow disc

within whose beam all's commonplace
and whose limits are described
by the whole night.

1967

Implosions[3]

The world's
not wanton
only wild and wavering [4]

I wanted to choose words that even you
would have to be changed by

Take the word
of my pulse, loving and ordinary
Send out your signals, hoist
your dark scribbled flags
but take
my hand

All wars are useless to the dead

My hands are knotted in the rope
and I cannot sound the bell

My hands are frozen to the switch
and I cannot throw it
The foot is in the wheel

When it's finished and we're lying
in a stubble of blistered flowers
eyes gaping, mouths staring
dusted with crushed arterial blues

I'll have done nothing
even for you?

1968

3. An implosion is a more or less violent
collapse inward.
4. The first three lines are stolen, by per-
mission, from Abbot Small [*Rich's note*].
Small was a student in one of the poet's
classes.

On Edges

When the ice starts to shiver
all across the reflecting basin
or water-lily leaves
dissect a simple surface
the word *drowning* flows through me.
You built a glassy floor
that held me
as I leaned to fish for old
hooks and toothed tin cans,
stems lashing out like ties of
silk dressing-gowns
archangels of lake-light
gripped in mud.

Now you hand me a torn letter.
On my knees, in the ashes, I could never
fit these ripped-up flakes together.
In the taxi I am still piecing
what syllables I can
translating at top speed like a thinking machine
that types out *useless* as *monster*
and *history* as *lampshade*.
Crossing the bridge I need all my nerve
to trust to the man-made cables.

The blades on that machine
could cut you to ribbons
but its function is humane.
Is this all I can say of these
delicate hooks, scythe-curved intentions
you and I handle? I'd rather
taste blood, yours or mine, flowing
from a sudden slash, than cut all day
with blunt scissors on dotted lines
like the teacher told.

1968

The Observer [5]

Completely protected on all sides
by volcanoes
a woman, darkhaired, in stained jeans
sleeps in central Africa.
In her dreams, her notebooks, still
private as maiden diaries,
the mountain gorillas move through their life term;
their gentleness survives
observation. Six bands of them
inhabit, with her, the wooded highland.
When I lay me down to sleep
unsheltered by any natural guardians
from the panicky life-cycle of my tribe
I wake in the old cellblock
observing the daily executions,
rehearsing the laws
I cannot subscribe to,
envying the pale gorilla-scented dawn
she wakes into, the stream where she washes her hair,
the camera-flash of her quiet
eye.

1968

Nightbreak

Something broken   Something
I need   By someone
I love   Next year
will I remember what
This anger   unreal
                              yet
has to be gone through
The sun to set
on this anger [6]
                        I go on
head down   into it

5. Suggested by a brief newspaper account of the fieldwork of Diane Fossey [*Rich's note*].
6. St. Paul's Epistle to the Ephesians, 4:26–27: "Never let the sun set on your anger or else you will give the devil a foothold."

The mountain pulsing
Into the oildrum   drops
the ball of fire.

Time is quiet   doesn't break things
or even wound   Things are in danger
from people   The frail clay lamps
of Mesopotamia[7]
row on row under glass
in the ethnological section
little hollows for dried-
up oil   The refugees
with their identical
tales of escape   I don't
collect what I can't use   I need
what can be broken.

In the bed the pieces fly together
and the rifts fill   or else
my body is a list   of wounds
symmetrically placed
a village
blown open   by planes
that did not   finish the job
The enemy has   withdrawn
between raids   become invisible
there are
            no agencies
                        of relief
the darkness becomes utter
Sleep   cracked and flaking
sifts over the shaken   target

What breaks   is night
not day   The white
scar   splitting
over the east
The crack weeping
Time for the pieces
                        to move
dumbly back
            toward each other.

1968

7. The ancient country between the Tigris and the Euphrates rivers.

From *The Will to Change*
(1971)

Planetarium

Thinking of Caroline Herschel (1750–1848)
astronomer, sister of William; [1] *and others.*

A woman in the shape of a monster
a monster in the shape of a woman
the skies are full of them

a woman   'in the snow
among the Clocks and instruments
or measuring the ground with poles'
in her 98 years to discover
8 comets

she whom the moon ruled
like us
levitating into the night sky
riding the polished lenses

Galaxies of women, there
doing penance for impetuousness
ribs chilled
in those spaces   of the mind

An eye,

                    'virile, precise and absolutely certain' [2]
                    from the mad webs of Uranusborg [3]

                                    encountering the NOVA

1. In helping her brother William (1738–1822), the discoverer of Uranus, Carolyn Herschel became a superb astronomer in her own right.
2. Uranienborg, "castle in the sky," was the name of the observatory built in 1576 by Tycho Brache (1546–1601), the Danish astronomer.
3. Brache, on November 11, 1573, discovered the famous "New Star" in the constellation Cassiopeia.

every impulse of light exploding
from the core
as life flies out of us

Tycho whispering at last
'Let me not seem to have lived in vain'[4]

What we see, we see
and seeing is changing

the light that shrivels a mountain
and leaves a man alive

Heartbeat of the pulsar[5]
heart sweating through my body

The radio impulse
pouring in from Taurus[6]

I am bombarded yet   I stand

I have been standing all my life in the
direct path of a battery of signals
the most accurately transmitted most
untranslatable language in the universe
I am a galactic[7] cloud so deep   so invo-
luted that a light wave could take 15
years to travel through me   And has
taken   I am an instrument in the shape
of a woman trying to translate pulsations
into images   for the relief of the body
and the reconstruction of the mind.

1968

4. Tycho Brache's last words.
5. Any of several very short-period variable galactic radio sources.
6. A constellation in the Northern Hemisphere near Orion and Aries.
7. Of, pertaining to, occurring in, or originating in the Milky Way.

the clot and fissure
of it appears
words of a man
in pain
a naked word
entering the clot
a hand grasping
through bars:

deliverance

What happens between us
has happened for centuries
we know it from literature

still it happens

sexual jealousy
outflung hand
beating bed

dryness of mouth
after panting

there are books that describe all this
and they are useless

You walk into the woods behind a house
there in that country
you find a temple
built eighteen hundred years ago
you enter without knowing
what it is you enter

so it is with us

no one knows what may happen
though the books tell everything

burn the texts   said Artaud[6]

---

6. Antonin Artaud (1896–1948), French
surrealist poet who called for the destruc-
tion of our present social thought pat-
terns. The phrase "burn the texts" is
quoted by Julian Beck in a section of
"Can Art Transform the World?" It ap-
pears as section 50 in Beck's *The Life
of the Theatre* (San Francisco, 1972).

5. I am composing on the typewriter late at night, thinking of today. How well we all spoke. A language is a map of our failures. Frederick Douglass wrote an English purer than Milton's.[7] People suffer highly in poverty. There are methods but we do not use them. Joan, who could not read, spoke some peasant form of French. Some of the suffering are: it is hard to tell the truth; this is America; I cannot touch you now. In America we have only the present tense. I am in danger. You are in danger. The burning of a book arouses no sensation in me. I know it hurts to burn. There are flames of napalm in Catonsville, Maryland. I know it hurts to burn. The typewriter is overheated, my mouth is burning, I cannot touch you and this is the oppressor's language.

1968

I Dream I'm the Death of Orpheus[8]

I am walking rapidly through striations of light and dark thrown
    under an arcade.

I am a woman in the prime of life, with certain powers
and those powers severely limited
by authorities whose faces I rarely see.
I am a woman in the prime of life
driving her dead poet in a black Rolls-Royce
through a landscape of twilight and thorns.
A woman with a certain mission
which if obeyed to the letter will leave her intact.
A woman with the nerves of a panther
a woman with contacts among Hell's Angels[9]
a woman feeling the fullness of her powers
at the precise moment when she must not use them
a woman sworn to lucidity
who sees through the mayhem, the smoky fires

7. Frederick Douglass (1817?–1895): American black abolitionist. Son of a slave woman, he escaped to the North and became a strong voice against slavery; he wrote *Narrative of The Life of Frederick Douglass* (1845, revised 1855). John Milton (1608–1674), English poet.

8. A legendary Thracian poet who descended to the underworld to recover his dead wife, Eurydice. Jean Cocteau (1889–1963) wrote and directed a motion picture, *Orphée* (1950), modernizing the story. Scenes and images from the movie are used in the poem. Death, a woman riding in a Rolls Royce guarded by motorcyclists with black leather jackets, comes for Orpheus and carries him through a mirror into the underworld on the other side.

9. A motorcycle club that originated in Oakland, California.

of these underground streets
her dead poet learning to walk backward against the wind
on the wrong side of the mirror

1968

Images for Godard[1]

1. Language as city:: Wittgenstein:[2]
   Driving to the limits
   of the city of words

   the superhighway streams
   like a comic strip

   to newer suburbs
   casements of shockproof glass

   where no one yet looks out
   or toward the coast where even now

   the squatters in their shacks
   await eviction

   When all conversation
   becomes an interview
   under duress

   when we come to the limits
   of the city

   my face must have a meaning

2. To know the extremes of light
   I sit in this darkness

   To see the present flashing
   in a rearview mirror

1. Jean-Luc Godard (1930–   ), semi-surrealist French writer and film director.
2. "Our language can be seen as an ancient city: a maze of little streets and squares, of old and new houses with additions from various periods; and this surrounded by a multitude of new boroughs with straight regular streets and uniform houses": Ludwig Wittgenstein (1889–1957), *Philosophical Investigations* (New York, 1958), p. 8.

blued in a plateglass pane
reddened in the reflection

of the red Triomphe[3]
parked at the edge of the sea

the sea glittering in the sun
the swirls of nebula

in the espresso cup
raindrops, neon spectra

on a vinyl raincoat

3. To love, to move perpetually
   as the body changes

   a dozen times a day
   the temperature of the skin

   the feeling of rise & fall
   deadweight & buoyancy

   the eye sunk inward
   the eye bleeding with speech

   *for that moment at least
   I wás you—*

   To be stopped, to shoot the same scene
   over & over

4. At the end of *Alphaville*[4]
   she says *I love you*

   and the film begins
   that you've said you'd never make

   because it's impossible:
   *things as difficult to show
   as horror & war & sickness are*[5]

---

3. A sports car.
4. A Godard movie produced in 1965.

5. A statement made by Godard in an interview.

meaning: *love,*
to speak in the mouth

to touch the breast
for a woman

to know the sex of a man
That film begins here

yet you don't show it
we leave the theatre

suffering from that

5. Interior monologue of the poet:
the notes for the poem are the only poem

the mind collecting, devouring
all these destructibles

the unmade studio couch the air
shifting the abalone shells

the mind of the poet is the only poem
the poet is at the movies
dreaming the film-maker's dream but differently
free in the dark as if asleep

free in the dusty beam of the projector
the mind of the poet is changing

the moment of change is the only poem

1970

A Valediction
Forbidding Mourning[6]

My swirling wants. Your frozen lips.
The grammar turned and attacked me.

6. This is also the title of a poem by the English metaphysical poet John Donne (1572–1631), written to his wife on the occasion of a trip to the Continent, during which he would be separated from her.

Themes, written under duress.
Emptiness of the notations.

They gave me a drug that slowed the healing of wounds.

I want you to see this before I leave:
the experience of repetition as death
the failure of criticism to locate the pain
the poster in the bus that said:
my bleeding is under control.

A red plant in a cemetery of plastic wreaths.

A last attempt: the language is a dialect called metaphor.
These images go unglossed: hair, glacier, flashlight.
When I think of a landscape I am thinking of a time.
When I talk of taking a trip I mean forever.
I could say: those mountains have a meaning
but further than that I could not say.

To do something very common, in my own way.

1970

Shooting Script
(11/69–7/70)[7]

PART I 11/69–2/70

1.

We were bound on the wheel of an endless conversation.

Inside this shell, a tide waiting for someone to enter.

A monologue waiting for you to interrupt it.

A man wading into the surf. The dialogue of the rock with the breaker.

---

7. Sections 1, 8, 13, and 14 are reprinted here.

The wave changed instantly by the rock; the rock changed by the wave returning over and over.

The dialogue that lasts all night or a whole lifetime.

A conversation of sounds melting constantly into rhythms.

A shell waiting for you to listen.

A tide that ebbs and flows against a deserted continent.

A cycle whose rhythm begins to change the meanings of words.

A wheel of blinding waves of light, the spokes pulsing out from where we hang together in the turning of an endless conversation.

The meaning that searches for its word like a hermit crab.

A monologue that waits for one listener.

An ear filled with one sound only.

A shell penetrated by meaning.

PART II 3–7/70

8.

—for Hugh Seidman

A woman waking behind grimed blinds slatted across a courtyard she never looks into.

Thinking of the force of a waterfall, the slash of cold air from the thickest water of the falls, slicing the green and ochre afternoon in which he turns his head and walks away.

Thinking of that place as an existence.

A woman reaching for the glass of water left all night on the bureau, the half-done poem, the immediate relief.

Entering the poem as a method of leaving the room.

Entering the paper airplane of the poem, which somewhere before its destination starts curling into ash and comes apart.

The woman is too heavy for the poem, she is a swollenness, a foot, an arm, gone asleep, grown absurd and out of bounds.

Rooted to memory like a wedge in a block of wood; she takes the pressure of her thought but cannot resist it.

You call this a poetry of false problems, the shotgun wedding of the mind, the subversion of choice by language.

Instead of the alternative: to pull the sooty strings to set the window bare to purge the room with light to feel the sun breaking in on the courtyard and the steamheat smothering in the shut-off pipes.

To feel existence as this time, this place, the pathos and force of the lumps of snow gritted and melting in the unloved corners of the courtyard.

13.

We are driven to odd attempts; once it would not have occurred to me to put out in a boat, not on a night like this.

Still, it was an instrument, and I had pledged myself to try any instrument that came my way. Never to refuse one from conviction of incompetence.

A long time I was simply learning to handle the skiff; I had no special training and my own training was against me.

I had always heard that darkness and water were a threat.

In spite of this, darkness and water helped me to arrive here.

I watched the lights on the shore I had left for a long time; each one, it seemed to me, was a light I might have lit, in the old days.

14.

Whatever it was: the grains of the glacier caked in the boot-cleats; ashes spilled on white formica.

The death-col viewed through power-glasses; the cube of ice melting on stainless steel.

Whatever it was, the image that stopped you, the one on which you came to grief, projecting it over & over on empty walls.

Now to give up the temptations of the projector; to see instead the web of cracks filtering across the plaster.

To read there the map of the future, the roads radiating from the initial split, the filaments thrown out from that impasse.

To reread the instructions on your palm; to find there how the lifeline, broken, keeps its direction.

To read the etched rays of the bullet-hole left years ago in the glass; to know in every distortion of the light what fracture is.

To put the prism in your pocket, the thin glass lens, the map of the inner city, the little book with gridded pages.

To pull yourself up by your own roots; to eat the last meal in your old neighborhood.

From *Diving into the Wreck*
(1973)

Trying to Talk with a Man

Out in this desert we are testing bombs,

that's why we came here.

Sometimes I feel an underground river
forcing its way between deformed cliffs
an acute angle of understanding
moving itself like a locus[1] of the sun
into this condemned scenery.

What we've had to give up to get here—
whole LP collections, films we starred in
playing in the neighborhoods, bakery windows
dull of dry, chocolate-filled Jewish cookies,
the language of love-letters, of suicide notes,
afternoons on the riverbank
pretending to be children

Coming out to this desert
we meant to change the face of
driving among dull green succulents
walking at noon in the ghost town
surrounded by a silence

that sounds like the silence of the place
except that it came with us
and is familiar
and everything we were saying until now
was an effort to blot it out—
coming out here we are up against it

1. In geometry, the set or configuration of all points satisfying specified geometric conditions.

Out here I feel more helpless
with you than without you
You mention the danger
and list the equipment
we talk of people caring for each other
in emergencies—laceration, thirst—
but you look at me like an emergency

Your dry heat feels like power
your eyes are stars of a different magnitude
they reflect lights that spell out: EXIT
when you get up and pace the floor

talking of the danger
as if it were not ourselves
as if we were testing anything else.

1971

When We Dead Awaken[2]

—for E.Y.

Trying to tell you how
the anatomy of the park
through stained panes, the way
guerrillas are advancing
through minefields, the trash
burning endlessly in the dump
to return to heaven like a stain—
everything outside our skins is an image
of this affliction:
stones on my table, carried by hand
from scenes I trusted
souvenirs of what I once described
as happiness
everything outside my skin
speaks of the fault that sends me limping
even the scars of my decisions
even the sunblaze in the mica-vein
even you, fellow-creature, sister,

2. The title of the last play of Henrik Ibsen (1828–1906).

sitting across from me, dark with love,
working like me to pick apart
working with me to remake
this trailing knitted thing, this cloth of darkness,
this woman's garment, trying to save the skein.

2.

The fact of being separate
enters your livelihood like a piece of furniture
—a chest of seventeenth-century wood
from somewhere in the North.
It has a huge lock shaped like a woman's head
but the key has not been found.
In the compartments are other keys
to lost doors, an eye of glass.
Slowly you begin to add
things of your own.
You come and go reflected in its panels.
You give up keeping track of anniversaries,
you begin to write in your diaries
more honestly than ever.

3.

The lovely landscape of southern Ohio
betrayed by strip mining, the
thick gold band on the adulterer's finger
the blurred programs of the offshore pirate station
are causes for hesitation.
Here in the matrix of need and anger, the
disproof of what we thought possible
failures of medication
doubts of another's existence
—tell it over and over, the words
get thick with unmeaning—
yet never have we been closer to the truth
of the lies we were living, listen to me:
the faithfulness I can imagine would be a weed
flowering in tar, a blue energy piercing
the massed atoms of a bedrock disbelief.

1971

Waking in the Dark

1.

The thing that arrests me is
    how we are composed of molecules

    (he showed me the figure in the paving stones)

    arranged without our knowledge and consent

        like the wirephoto composed
        of millions of dots

            in which the man from Bangladesh[3]
            walks starving
                    on the front page
                    knowing nothing about it

        which is his presence for the world

2.

We were standing in line outside of something
two by two, or alone in pairs, or simply alone,
looking into windows full of scissors,
windows full of shoes. The street was closing,
the city was closing, would we be the lucky ones
to make it? They were showing
in a glass case, the Man Without A Country.[4]
We held up our passports in his face, we wept for him.

They are dumping animal blood into the sea
to bring up the sharks. Sometimes every
aperture of my body
leaks blood. I don't know whether
to pretend that this is natural.
Is there a law about this, a law of nature?
You worship the blood
you call it hysterical bleeding
you want to drink it like milk

3. Formerly East Pakistan, which broke
away from Pakistan on January 10, 1972.
It is one of the poorest and most popu-
lous states in the world.
4. A short story (1863) by Edward Everett

Hale (1822–1909) about a naval officer
who makes a hasty wish never to see
America again. It was made into an
opera by Walter Damrosch and produced
at the Metropolitan Opera in 1937.

you dip your finger into it and write
you faint at the smell of it
you dream of dumping me into the sea.

3.

The tragedy of sex
lies around us, a woodlot
the axes are sharpened for.
The old shelters and huts
stare through the clearing with a certain resolution
—the hermit's cabin, the hunters' shack—
scenes of masturbation
and dirty jokes.
A man's world. But finished.
They themselves have sold it to the machines.
I walk the unconscious forest,
a woman dressed in old army fatigues
that have shrunk to fit her, I am lost
at moments, I feel dazed
by the sun pawing between the trees,
cold in the bog and lichen of the thicket.
Nothing will save this. I am alone,
kicking the last rotting logs
with their strange smell of life, not death,
wondering what on earth it all might have become.

4.

Clarity,

            spray

blinding and purging

spears of sun striking the water

the bodies riding the air

like gliders

the bodies in slow motion

falling
into the pool
at the Berlin Olympics

control; loss of control

the bodies rising
arching back to the tower

time reeling backward

clarity of open air
before the dark chambers
with the shower-heads

the bodies falling again
freely

                    faster than light
the water opening
like air
like realization

A woman made this film
against

the law
of gravity

5.

All night dreaming of a body
space weighs on differently from mine
We are making love in the street
the traffic flows off from us
pouring back like a sheet
the asphalt stirs with tenderness
there is no dismay
we move together like underwater plants

Over and over, starting to wake
I dive back to discover you
still whispering, *touch me,* we go on
streaming through the slow
citylight forest ocean
stirring our body hair

But this is the saying of a dream
on waking
I wish there were somewhere
actual we could stand
handing the power-glasses back and forth
looking at the earth, the wildwood
where the split began

1971

Incipience [5]

1. To live, to lie awake
under scarred plaster
while ice is forming over the earth
at an hour when nothing can be done
to further any decision

to know the composing of the thread
inside the spider's body
first atoms of the web
visible tomorrow

to feel the fiery future
of every matchstick in the kitchen

Nothing can be done
but by inches. I write out my life
hour by hour, word by word
gazing into the anger of old women on the bus
numbering the striations
of air inside the ice cube
imagining the existence
of something uncreated
this poem
our lives

2. A man is asleep in the next room
    We are his dreams
    We have the heads and breasts of women
    the bodies of birds of prey
    Sometimes we turn into silver serpents
While we sit up smoking and talking of how to live
he turns on the bed and murmurs

A man is asleep in the next room
    A neurosurgeon enters his dream
    and begins to dissect his brain
    She does not look like a nurse
    she is absorbed in her work
    she has a stern, delicate face like Marie Curie [6]
She is not/might be either of us

5. An early or initial stage; the point of beginning to exist or appear.
6. Marie Curie (1867–1934): the Polish-born French chemist who discovered radium.

A man is asleep in the next room
    He has spent a whole day
    standing, throwing stones into the black pool
    which keeps its blackness
Outside the frame of his dream we are stumbling up the hill
    hand in hand, stumbling and guiding each other
    over the scarred volcanic rock

1971

The Stranger

Looking as I've looked before, straight down the heart
of the street to the river
walking the rivers of the avenues
feeling the shudder of the caves beneath the asphalt
watching the lights turn on in the towers
walking as I've walked before
like a man, like a woman, in the city
my visionary anger cleansing my sight
and the detailed perceptions of mercy
flowering from that anger

if I come into a room out of the sharp misty light
and hear them talking a dead language
if they ask me my identity
what can I say but
I am the androgyne[7]
I am the living mind you fail to describe
in your dead language
the lost noun, the verb surviving
only in the infinitive
the letters of my name are written under the lids
of the newborn child

1972

Diving into the Wreck

First having read the book of myths,
and loaded the camera,
and checked the edge of the knife-blade,

---

7. One whose psyche shows male and female characteristics.

I put on
the body-armor of black rubber
the absurd flippers
the grave and awkward mask.
I am having to do this
not like Cousteau[8] with his
assiduous team
aboard the sun-flooded schooner
but here alone.

There is a ladder.
The ladder is always there
hanging innocently
close to the side of the schooner.
We know what it is for,
we who have used it.
Otherwise
it's a piece of maritime floss
some sundry equipment.

I go down.
Rung after rung and still
the oxygen immerses me
the blue light
the clear atoms
of our human air.
I go down.
My flippers cripple me,
I crawl like an insect down the ladder
and there is no one
to tell me when the ocean
will begin.

First the air is blue and then
it is bluer and then green and then
black I am blacking out and yet
my mask is powerful
it pumps my blood with power
the sea is another story
the sea is not a question of power
I have to learn alone
to turn my body without force
in the deep element.

8. Jacques Cousteau (1910–   ): French underwater explorer and author.

And now: it is easy to forget
what I came for
among so many who have always
lived here
swaying their crenellated[9] fans
between the reefs
and besides
you breathe differently down here.

I came to explore the wreck.
The words are purposes.
The words are maps.
I came to see the damage that was done
and the treasures that prevail.
I stroke the beam of my lamp
slowly along the flank
of something more permanent
than fish or weed

the thing I came for:
the wreck and not the story of the wreck
the thing itself and not the myth

the drowned face always staring
toward the sun
the evidence of damage
worn by salt and sway into this threadbare beauty
the ribs of the disaster
curving their assertion
among the tentative haunters.

This is the place.
And I am here, the mermaid whose dark hair
streams black, the merman in his armored body
We circle silently
about the wreck
we dive into the hold.
I am she: I am he

whose drowned face sleeps with open eyes
whose breasts still bear the stress
whose silver, copper, vermeil[1] cargo lies
obscurely inside barrels

9. Notched with rounded or scalloped projections.

1. Gilded metal, such as silver, bronze, or copper.

half-wedged and left to rot
we are the half-destroyed instruments
that once held to a course
the water-eaten log
the fouled compass

We are, I am, you are
by cowardice or courage
the one who find our way
back to this scene
carrying a knife, a camera
a book of myths
in which
our names do not appear.

1972

The Phenomenology of Anger

1. The freedom of the wholly mad
to smear & play with her madness
write with her fingers dipped in it
the length of a room

which is not, of course, the freedom
you have, walking on Broadway
to stop & turn back or go on
10 blocks; 20 blocks

but feels enviable maybe
to the compromised

curled in the placenta of the real
which was to feed & which is strangling her.

2. Trying to light a log that's lain in the damp
as long as this house has stood:
even with dry sticks I can't get started
even with thorns.
I twist last year into a knot of old headlines
—this rose won't bloom.

How does a pile of rags the machinist wiped his hands on
feel in its cupboard, hour upon hour?
Each day during the heat-wave

they took the temperature of the haymow.
I huddled fugitive
in the warm sweet simmer of the hay

muttering: *Come.*

3. Flat heartland of winter.
The moonmen come back from the moon
the firemen come out of the fire.
Time without a taste: time without decisions.

Self-hatred, a monotone in the mind.
The shallowness of a life lived in exile
even in the hot countries.
Cleaver,[2] staring into a window full of knives.

4. White light splits the room.
Table. Window. Lampshade. You.

My hands, sticky in a new way.
Menstrual blood
seeming to leak from your side.

Will the judges try to tell me
which was the blood of whom?

5. Madness. Suicide. Murder.
Is there no way out but these?
The enemy, always just out of sight
snowshoeing the next forest, shrouded
in a snowy blur, abominable snowman
—at once the most destructive
and the most elusive being
gunning down the babies at My Lai
vanishing in the face of confrontation.

The prince of air and darkness
computing body counts, masturbating
in the factory
of facts.

6. Fantasies of murder: not enough:
to kill is to cut off from pain

2. Eldridge Cleaver (1935–   ): one of the theorists of the Black Panther Party who split with the party line by continuing to advocate violence. Refusing to serve a prison sentence for a crime of which he said he was not guilty, he escaped to exile in Algeria.
3. A village in South Vietnam whose inhabitants were massacred in March, 1968, by an American army platoon.

but the killer goes on hurting

Not enough. When I dream of meeting
the enemy, this is my dream:

white acetylene
ripples from my body
effortlessly released
perfectly trained
on the true enemy

raking his body down to the thread
of existence
burning away his lie
leaving him in a new
world; a changed
man

7. I suddenly see the world
as no longer viable:
you are out there burning the crops
with some new sublimate
This morning you left the bed
we still share
and went out to spread impotence
upon the world

I hate you.
I hate the mask you wear, your eyes
assuming a depth
they do not possess, drawing me
into the grotto of your skull
the landscape of bone
I hate your words
they make me think of fake
revolutionary bills
crisp imitation parchment
they sell at battlefields.

Last night, in this room, weeping
I asked you: *what are you feeling?*
do you feel anything?

Now in the torsion of your body
as you defoliate the fields we lived from
I have your answer.

8. Dogeared earth. Wormeaten moon.
A pale cross-hatching of silver
lies like a wire screen on the black
water. All these phenomena
are temporary.

I would have loved to live in a world
of women and men gaily
in collusion with green leaves, stalks,
building mineral cities, transparent domes,
little huts of woven grass
each with its own pattern—
a conspiracy to coexist
with the Crab Nebula,[4] the exploding
universe, the Mind—

9. *The only real love I have ever felt*
was for children and other women.
Everything else was lust, pity,
self-hatred, pity, lust.
This is a woman's confession.
Now, look again at the face
of Botticelli's[5] Venus, Kali,[6]
the Judith of Chartres[7]
with her so-called smile.

10. how we are burning up our lives
testimony:

> the subway
> hurtling to Brooklyn
> her head on her knees
> asleep or drugged

la vía del tren subterráneo
es peligrosa[8]

> many sleep
> the whole way

4. The Crab (also called Cancer) is a constellation in the Northern Hemisphere near Leo and Gemini. A nebula is any diffuse mass of interstellar dust, gas, or both.
5. Sandro Botticelli (1444?–1510), Italian painter whose *Birth of Venus* is now in the Uffizi Gallery, Florence.
6. Hindu goddess, wife of Shiva, often depicted dancing triumphantly on his body.
7. On the north portal of Chartres Cathedral is a series of scenes depicting Judith's decapitation of the Assyrian general Holofernes (*Book of Judith* 8–13).
8. Spanish for "the subway track is dangerous"—part of a sign printed in English and Spanish in New York City subways.

> others sit
> staring holes of fire into the air
> others plan rebellion:
> night after night
> awake in prison, my mind
> licked at the mattress like a flame
> till the cellblock went up roaring

Thoreau setting fire to the woods [9]

Every act of becoming conscious
(it says here in this book)
is an unnatural act

1972

Living in the Cave

Reading the Parable of the Cave [1]
while living in the cave,

> black moss

deadening my footsteps
candles stuck on rock-ledges
weakening my eyes

These things around me, with their
daily requirements:

> fill me, empty me
talk to me, warm me, let me
suck on you

Every one of them has a plan that depends on me

stalactites [2] want to become
stalagmites [3]
veins of ore
imagine their preciousness

9. Henry David Thoreau (1817–1862): American essayist and poet, author of *Walden*. Once Thoreau's campfire spread to the woods and threatened the town; his *Journal* describes the mixture of horror and fascination with which he watched it burn (*The Writings of Henry David Thoreau: Journal II*, ed. Bradford Torrey [Walden edition, Boston, 1906], pp. 21–26).

1. The Greek philosopher Plato (427?–347 B.C.) compared all human life to living in a cave (in his *Republic*, Book VII).
2. A cylindrical or conical deposit projecting downward from the roof of a cavern as a result of the dripping of mineral-rich water.
3. A similar deposit building upward from the cavern floor.

candles see themselves disembodied
into gas
and taking flight

the bat hangs dreaming
of an airy world

None of them, not one
sees me
as I see them

1972

The Ninth Symphony of Beethoven[4]
Understood at Last as a Sexual Message

A man in terror of impotence
or infertility, not knowing the difference
a man trying to tell something
howling from the climacteric[5]
music of the entirely
isolated soul
yelling at Joy from the tunnel of the ego
music without the ghost
of another person in it, music
trying to tell something the man
does not want out, would keep if he could
gagged and bound and flogged with chords of Joy
where everything is silence and the
beating of a bloody fist upon
a splintered table

1972

For the Dead

I dreamed I called you on the telephone
to say: *Be kinder to yourself*
but you were sick and would not answer

4. Ludwig van Beethoven (1770–1827):
German composer. His Ninth Symphony
climaxes in a choral "Hymn to Joy."
5. A period or year of life when physi-
ological changes take place in the body;
often a synonym for menopause in
women or decline in potency in men.

The waste of my love goes on this way
trying to save you from yourself

I have always wondered about the leftover
energy, water rushing down a hill
long after the rains have stopped

or the fire you want to go to bed from
but cannot leave, burning-down but not burnt-down
the red coals more extreme, more curious
in their flashing and dying
than you wish they were
sitting there long after midnight

1972

From a Survivor

The pact that we made was the ordinary pact
of men & women in those days

I don't know who we thought we were
that our personalities
could resist the failures of the race

Lucky or unlucky, we didn't know
the race had failures of that order
and that we were going to share them

Like everybody else, we thought of ourselves as special

Your body is as vivid to me
as it ever was: even more

since my feeling for it is clearer:
I know what it could and could not do

it is no longer
the body of a god
or anything with power over my life

Next year it would have been 20 years
and you are wastefully dead
who might have made the leap
we talked, too late, of making

which I live now
not as a leap
but a succession of brief, amazing movements

each one making possible the next

1972

From *Poems: Selected and New*
(1975)

From an Old House in America

1.

Deliberately, long ago
the carcasses

of old bugs crumbled
into the rut of the window

and we started sleeping here
Fresh June bugs batter this June's

screens, June-lightning batters
the spiderweb

I sweep the wood-dust
from the wood-box

the snout of the vacuum cleaner
sucks the past away

2.

Other lives were lived here:
mostly un-articulate

yet someone left her creamy signature
in the trail of rusticated

narcissus straggling up
through meadowgrass and vetch[1]

Families breathed close
boxed-in from the cold

1. A climbing plant of the genus vicia.

hard times, short growing season
the old rainwater cistern

hulks in the cellar

3.

Like turning through the contents of a drawer:
these rusted screws, this empty vial

useless, this box of watercolor paints
dried to insolubility—

but this—
this pack of cards with no card missing

still playable
and three good fuses

and this toy: a little truck
scarred red, yet all its wheels still turn

The humble tenacity of things
waiting for people, waiting for months, for years

4.

Often rebuked, yet always back returning[2]
I place my hand on the hand

of the dead, invisible palm-print
on the doorframe

spiked with daylilies, green leaves
catching in the screen door

or I read the backs of old postcards
curling from thumbtacks, winter and summer

fading through cobweb-tinted panes—
white church in Norway

Dutch hyacinths bleeding azure
red beach on Corsica

---

2. Borrowed from a poem, "Stanzas," by Emily Brontë [*Rich's note*].

set-pieces of the world
stuck to this house of plank

I flash on wife and husband
embattled, in the years

that dried, dim ink was wet
those signatures

5.

If they call me man-hater, you
would have known it for a lie

but the *you* I want to speak to
has become your death

If I dream of you these days
I know my dreams are mine and not of you

yet something hangs between us
older and stranger than ourselves

like a translucent curtain, a sheet of water
a dusty window

the irreducible, incomplete connection
between the dead and living

or between man and woman in this
savagely fathered and unmothered world

6.

The other side of a translucent
curtain, a sheet of water

a dusty window, Non-being
utters its flat tones

the speech of an actor learning his lines
phonetically

the final autistic[3] statement
of the self-destroyer

---

3. The word describes a person in a state of abnormal subjectivity and withdrawal.

All my energy reaches out tonight
to comprehend a miracle beyond

raising the dead: the undead to watch
back on the road of birth

7.

I am an American woman:
I turn that over

like a leaf pressed in a book
I stop and look up from

into the coals of the stove
or the black square of the window

Foot-slogging through the Bering Strait[4]
jumping from the *Arbella*[5] to my death

chained to the corpse beside me[6]
I feel my pains begin

I am washed up on this continent
shipped here to be fruitful

my body a hollow ship
bearing sons to the wilderness

sons who ride away
on horseback, daughters

whose juices drain like mine
into the *arroyo*[7] of stillbirths, massacres

4. The body of water lying between Alaska and the Kamchatka Peninsula of the U.S.S.R. Anthropologists surmise that the ancestors of the American Indians came from the Asian continent by this route when the land masses of Asia and North America were still joined.
5. Ship in which the Puritans, under the leadership of William Bradford (1590?–1657), came to New England. Anne Bradstreet (1612?–1672), the first woman poet in America, was on board. Her collection of verse, *The Tenth Muse* (1650), is the first book of poems written in the New World.
6. Many African women went into labor and gave birth on the slave-ships of the Middle Passage, chained for the duration of the voyage to the dying or the dead [*Rich's note*].
7. A deep gully cut by an intermittent stream; a dry gulch.

Hanged as witches, sold as breeding-wenches
my sisters leave me

I am not the wheatfield
nor the virgin forest

I never chose this place
yet I am of it now

In my decent collar, in the daguerrotype[8]
I pierce its legend with my look

my hands wring the necks of prairie chickens
I am used to blood

When the men hit the hobo track
I stay on with the children

my power is brief and local
but I know my power

I have lived in isolation
from other women, so much

in the mining camps, the first cities
the Great Plains winters

Most of the time, in my sex, I was alone

8.

Tonight in this northeast kingdom
striated iris stand in a jar with daisies

the porcupine gnaws in the shed
fireflies beat and simmer

caterpillars begin again
their long, innocent climb

the length of leaves of burdock
or webbing of a garden chair

---

8. An early photographic process, or a photograph made by this process.

plain and ordinary things
speak softly

the light square on old wallpaper
where a poster has fallen down

Robert Indiana's LOVE[9]
leftover of a decade[1]

9.

I do not want to simplify
Or: I would simplify

by naming the complexity
It was made over-simple all along

the separation of powers
the allotment of sufferings

her spine cracking in labor
his plow driving across the Indian graves

her hand unconscious on the cradle, her mind
with the wild geese

his mother-hatred driving him
into exile from the earth

the refugee couple with their cardboard luggage
standing on the ramshackle landing-stage

he with fingers frozen around his Law
she with her down quilt sewn through iron nights

—the weight of the old world, plucked
drags after them, a random feather-bed

10.

Her children dead of diphtheria, she
set herself on fire with kerosene

9. Robert Indiana, pseudonym of Robert Clark (1928–   ), American artist, whose pop painting *LOVE* is a brightly colored arrangement of the letters of the word in capitals.
1. The decade of the sixties.

(O Lord I was unworthy
Thou didst find me out)

she left the kitchen scrubbed
down to the marrow of its boards[2]

"The penalty for barrenness
is emptiness

my punishment is my crime
what I have failed to do, is me . . ."

—Another month without a show
and this the seventh year[3]

O Father let this thing pass out of me
I swear to You

I will live for the others, asking nothing
I will ask nothing, ever, for myself

11.

Out back of this old house
datura[4] tangles with a gentler weed

its spiked pods smelling
of bad dreams and death

I reach through the dark, groping
past spines of nightmare

to brush the leaves of sensuality
A dream of tenderness

wrestles with all I know of history
I cannot now lie down

with a man who fears my power
or reaches for me as for death

2. Based on incidents described by Michael Lesy in *Wisconsin Death Trip* (New York, 1973).
3. The speaker in these lines suffers from her barrenness as the one in the next four does from repeated pregnancies.
4. A poisonous hallucinogenic weed. It has a spiky green pod and a white flower, and is also known as jimson-weed, or deadly nightshade [*Rich's note*].

or with a lover who imagines
we are not in danger

12.

If it was lust that had defined us—
their lust and fear of our deep places

we have done our time
as faceless torsos licked by fire

we are in the open, on our way—
our counterparts

the pinyon jay, the small
gilt-winged insect

the Cessna⁵ throbbing level
the raven floating in the gorge

the rose and violet vulva of the earth
filling with darkness

yet deep within a single sparkle
of red, a human fire

and near and yet above the western planet
calmly biding her time

13.

They were the distractions, lust and fear
but are

themselves a key
Everything that can be used, will be:

the fathers in their ceremonies
the genital contests

the cleansing of blood from pubic hair
the placenta buried and guarded

their terror of blinding
by the look of her who bore them

5. A light airplane.

If you do not believe
that fear and hatred

read the lesson again
in the old dialect

14.

But can't you see me as a human being
he said

What is a human being
she said

I try to understand
he said

what will you undertake
she said

will you punish me for history
he said

what will you undertake
she said

do you believe in collective guilt
he said

let me look in your eyes
she said

15.

Who is here. The Erinyes.[6]
One to sit in judgment.

One to speak tenderness.
One to inscribe the verdict on the canyon wall.

If you have not confessed
the damage

---

6. Greek goddesses of vengeance (the Furies).

if you have not recognized
the Mother of reparations

if you have not come to terms
with the women in the mirror

if you have not come to terms
with the inscription

the terms of the ordeal
the discipline   the verdict

if still you are on your way
still She awaits your coming

16.

"Such women are dangerous
to the order of things"

and yes, we will be dangerous
to ourselves

groping through spines of nightmare
(*datura* tangling with a simpler herb)

because the line dividing
lucidity from darkness

is yet to be marked out

Isolation, the dream
of the frontier woman

leveling her rifle along
the homestead fence

still snares our pride
—a suicidal leaf

laid under the burning-glass
in the sun's eye

Any woman's death diminishes me

1974

The Poet on Her Work

[Poetry and Experience: Statement at a Poetry Reading] (1964) †

What a poem used to be for me, what it is today.

In the period in which my first two books were written I had a much more absolutist approach to the universe than I now have. I also felt—as many people still feel—that a poem was an arrangement of ideas and feelings, pre-determined, and it said what I had already decided it should say. There were occasional surprises, occasions of happy discovery that an unexpected turn could be taken, but control, technical mastery and intellectual clarity were the real goals, and for many reasons it was satisfying to be able to create this kind of formal order in poems.

Only gradually, within the last five or six years, did I begin to feel that these poems, even the ones I liked best and in which I felt I'd said most, were queerly limited; that in many cases I had suppressed, omitted, falsified even, certain disturbing elements, to gain that perfection of order. Perhaps this feeling began to show itself in a poem like "Rural Reflections," in which there is an awareness already that experience is always greater and more unclassifiable than we give it credit for being.

Today, I have to say that what I know I know through making poems. Like the novelist who finds that his characters begin to have a life of their own and to demand certain experiences, I find that I can no longer go to write a poem with a neat handful of materials and express those materials according to a prior plan: the poem itself engenders new sensations, new awareness in me as it progresses. Without for one moment turning my back on conscious choice and selection, I have been increasingly willing to let the unconscious offer its materials, to listen to more than the one voice of a single idea. Perhaps a simple way of putting it would be to say that instead of poems *about* experiences I am getting poems that *are* experiences, that contribute to my knowledge and my emotional life even while they reflect and assimilate it. In my earlier poems I told you, as precisely and eloquently as I knew how, about something; in the more recent poems something is happening, something has happened to me and, if I have been a good parent to the poem, something will happen to you who read it.

† Quoted in "Adrienne Rich: The Poetics of Change," by Albert Gelpi, in *American Poetry Since 1960*, edited by Robert B. Shaw (Cheadle, Cheshire: Carcanet Press Ltd., 1973), pp. 132–133. Reprinted by permission of the publisher.

When We Dead Awaken: Writing as Re-Vision
(1971) †

Ibsen's *When We Dead Awaken* is a play about the use that the
male artist and thinker—in the process of creating culture as we
know it—has made of women, in his life and in his work; and about
a woman's slow struggling awakening to the use to which her life
has been put. Bernard Shaw wrote in 1900 of this play:

> [Ibsen] shows us that no degradation ever devized or permitted
> is as disastrous as this degradation; that through it women can die
> into luxuries for men and yet can kill them; that men and women
> are becoming conscious of this; and that what remains to be seen
> as perhaps the most interesting of all imminent social develop-
> ments is what will happen "when we dead awaken".[1]

It's exhilarating to be alive in a time of awakening consciousness;
it can also be confusing, disorienting, and painful. This awakening
of dead or sleeping consciousness has already affected the lives of
millions of women, even those who don't know it yet. It is also af-
fecting the lives of men, even those who deny its claims upon them.
The argument will go on whether an oppressive economic class sys-
tem is responsible for the oppressive nature of male/female rela-
tions, or whether, in fact, the sexual class system is the original
model on which all the others are based. But in the last few years
connections have been drawn between our sexual lives and our po-
litical institutions, which are inescapable and illuminating. The
sleepwalkers are coming awake, and for the first time this awaken-
ing has a collective reality; it is no longer such a lonely thing to
open one's eyes.

Re-vision—the act of looking back, of seeing with fresh eyes, of
entering an old text from a new critical direction—is for us more
than a chapter in cultural history: it is an act of survival. Until we
can understand the assumptions in which we are drenched we can-
not know ourselves. And this drive to self-knowledge, for woman,
is more than a search for identity: it is part of her refusal of the self-
destructiveness of male-dominated society. A radical critique of lit-
erature, feminist in its impulse, would take the work first of all as
a clue to how we live, how we have been living, how we have been
led to imagine ourselves, how our language has trapped as well as
liberated us; and how we can begin to see—and therefore live—
afresh. A change in the concept of sexual identity is essential if we

† From *College English*, XXXIV, 1 (Oc-
tober, 1972), 18–25. Copyright © 1972
by the National Council of Teachers of
English. Reprinted by permission of the
publisher and the author.

1. G. B. Shaw, *The Quintessence of Ib-
senism* (Hill and Wang, 1922), p. 139
[*Rich's note*].

are not going to see the old political order re-assert itself in every new revolution. We need to know the writing of the past, and know it differently than we have ever known it; not to pass on a tradition but to break its hold over us.

For writers, and at this moment for women writers in particular, there is the challenge and promise of a whole new psychic geography to be explored. But there is also a difficult and dangerous walking on the ice, as we try to find language and images for a consciousness we are just coming into, and with little in the past to support us. I want to talk about some apects of this difficulty and this danger.

Jane Harrison, the great classical anthropologist, wrote in 1914 in a letter to her friend Gilbert Murray:

> By the by, about "Women," it has bothered me often—why do women never want to write poetry about Man as a sex—why is Woman a dream and a terror to man and not the other way around? . . . Is it mere convention and propriety, or something deeper? [2]

I think Jane Harrison's question cuts deep into the myth-making tradition, the romantic tradition; deep into what women and men have been to each other; and deep into the psyche of the woman writer. Thinking about that question, I began thinking of the work of two 20th-century women poets, Sylvia Plath and Diane Wakoski. It strikes me that in the work of both Man appears as, if not a dream, a fascination and a terror; and that the source of the fascination and the terror is, simply, Man's power—to dominate, tyrannize, choose, or reject the woman. The charisma of Man seems to come purely from his power over her and his control of the world by force, not from anything fertile or life-giving in him. And, in the work of both these poets, it is finally the woman's sense of *herself*—embattled, possessed—that gives the poetry its dynamic charge, its rhythms of struggle, need, will, and female energy. Convention and propriety are perhaps not the right words, but until recently this female anger and this furious awareness of the Man's power over her were not available materials to the female poet, who tended to write of Love as the source of her suffering, and to view that victimization by Love as an almost inevitable fate. Or, like Marianne Moore and Elizabeth Bishop, she kept human sexual relationships at a measured and chiselled distance in her poems.

One answer to Jane Harrison's question has to be that historically men and women have played very different parts in each others'

2. J. G. Stewart, *Jane Ellen Harrison: A Portrait from Letters* (London, 1959), p. 140 [*Rich's note*].

lives. Where woman has been a luxury for man, and has served as
the painter's model and the poet's muse, but also as comforter,
nurse, cook, bearer of his seed, secretarial assistant and copyist of
manuscripts, man has played a quite different role for the female
artist. Henry James repeats an incident which the writer Prosper
Mérimée described, of how, while he was living with George Sand,

> he once opened his eyes, in the raw winter dawn, to see his com-
> panion, in a dressing-gown, on her knees before the domestic
> hearth, a candlestick beside her and a red *madras* round her head,
> making bravely, with her own hands, the fire that was to enable
> her to sit down betimes to urgent pen and paper. The story rep-
> resents him as having felt that the spectacle chilled his ardor and
> tried his taste; her appearance was unfortunate, her occupation
> an inconsequence, and her industry a reproof—the result of all
> of which was a lively irritation and an early rupture.[3]

I am suggesting that the specter of this kind of male judgment, along
with the active discouragement and thwarting of her needs by a cul-
ture controlled by males, has created problems for the woman
writer: problems of contact with herself, problems of language and
style, problems of energy and survival.

In rereading Virginia Woolf's *A Room Of One's Own* for the first
time in some years, I was astonished at the sense of effort, of pains
taken, of dogged tentativeness in the tone of that essay. And I
recognized that tone. I had heard it often enough, in myself and in
other women. It is the tone of a woman almost in touch with her
anger, who is determined not to appear angry, who is *willing* her-
self to be calm, detached, and even charming in a roomful of men
where things have been said which are attacks on her very integrity.
Virginia Woolf is addressing an audience of women, but she is
acutely conscious—as she always was—of being overheard by men:
by Morgan and Lytton and Maynard Keynes and for that matter
by her father, Leslie Stephen. She drew the language out into an
exacerbated thread in her determination to have her own sensibility
yet protect it from those masculine presences. Only at rare moments
in that essay do you hear the passion in her voice; she was trying to
sound as cool as Jane Austen, as Olympian as Shakespeare, because
that is the way the men of the culture thought a writer should
sound.

No male writer has written primarily or even largely for women,
or with the sense of women's criticism as a consideration when he
chooses his materials, his theme, his language. But to a lesser or
greater extent, every woman writer has written for men even when,

3. Henry James, "Notes on Novelists" in *Selected Literary Criticism of Henry James,* ed. Morris Shapira (London: Heineman, 1963), pp. 157–58 [*Rich's note*].

like Virginia Woolf, she was supposed to be addressing women. If we have come to the point when this balance might begin to change, when women can stop being haunted, not only by "convention and propriety" but by internalized fears of being and saying themselves, then it is an extraordinary moment for the women writer—and reader.

I have hesitated to do what I am going to do now, which is to use myself as an illustration. For one thing, it's a lot easier and less dangerous to talk about other women writers. But there is something else. Like Virginia Woolf, I am aware of the women who are not with us here because they are washing the dishes and looking after the children. Nearly fifty years after she spoke, that fact remains largely unchanged. And I am thinking also of women whom she left out of the picture altogether—women who are washing other people's dishes and caring for other people's children, not to mention women who went on the streets last night in order to feed their children. We seem to be special women here, we have liked to think of ourselves as special, and we have known that men would tolerate, even romanticize us as special, as long as our words and actions didn't threaten their privilege of tolerating or rejecting us according to *their* ideas of what a special woman ought to be. An important insight of the radical women's movement, for me, has been how divisive and how ultimately destructive is this myth of the special woman, who is also the token woman. Every one of us here in this room has had great luck—we are teachers, writers, academicians; our own gifts could not have been enough, for we all know women whose gifts are buried or aborted. Our struggles can have meaning only if they can help to change the lives of women whose gifts— and whose very being—continue to be thwarted.

My own luck was being born white and middle-class into a house full of books, with a father who encouraged me to read and write. So for about twenty years I wrote for a particular man, who criticized and praised me and made me feel I was indeed "special." The obverse side of this, of course, was that I tried for a long time to please him, or rather, not to displease him. And then of course there were other men—writers, teachers—the Man, who was not a terror or a dream but a literary master and a master in other ways less easy to acknowledge. And there were all those poems about women, written by men: it seemed to be a given that men wrote poems and women frequently inhabited them. These women were almost always beautiful, but threatened with the loss of beauty, the loss of youth—the fate worse than death. Or, they were beautiful and died young, like Lucy and Lenore. Or, the woman was like Maud Gonne, cruel and disastrously mistaken, and the poem reproached her because she had refused to become a luxury for the poet.

A lot is being said today about the influence that the myths and images of women have on all of us who are products of culture. I think it has been a peculiar confusion to the girl or woman who tries to write because she is peculiarly susceptible to language. She goes to poetry or fiction looking for *her* way of being in the world, since she too has been putting words and images together; she is looking eagerly for guides, maps, possibilities; and over and over in the "words' masculine persuasive force" of literature she comes up against something that negates everything she is about: she meets the image of Woman in books written by men. She finds a terror and a dream, she finds a beautiful pale face, she finds La Belle Dame Sans Merci, she finds Juliet or Tess or Salomé, but precisely what she does not find is that absorbed, drudging, puzzled, sometimes inspired creature, herself, who sits at a desk trying to put words together.

So what does she do? What did I do? I read the older women poets with their peculiar keenness and ambivalence: Sappho, Christina Rossetti, Emily Dickinson, Elinor Wylie, Edna Millay, H.D. I discovered that the woman poet most admired at the time (by men) was Marianne Moore, who was maidenly, elegant, intellectual, discreet. But even in reading these women I was looking in them for the same things I had found in the poetry of men, because I wanted women poets to be the equals of men, and to be equal was still confused with sounding the same.

I know that my style was formed first by male poets: by the men I was reading as an undergraduate—Frost, Dylan Thomas, Donne, Auden, MacNiece, Stevens, Yeats. What I chiefly learned from them was craft. But poems are like dreams: in them you put what you don't know you know. Looking back at poems I wrote before I was 21, I'm startled because beneath the conscious craft are glimpses of the split I even then experienced between the girl who wrote poems, who defined herself in writing poems, and the girl who was to define herself by her relationships with men. "Aunt Jennifer's Tigers," [4] written while I was a student, looks with deliberate detachment at this split. In writing this poem, composed and apparently cool as it is, I thought I was creating a portrait of an imaginary woman. But this woman suffers from the opposition of her imagination, worked out in tapestry, and her life-style, "ringed with ordeals she was mastered by." It was important to me that Aunt Jennifer was a person as distinct from myself as possible—distanced by the formalism of the poem, by its objective, observant tone—even by putting the woman in a different generation.

In those years formalism was part of the strategy—like asbestos gloves, it allowed me to handle materials I couldn't pick up bare-

4. See p. 2, above.

handed. (A later strategy was to use the persona of a man, as I did in "The Loser.") I finished college, published my first book by a fluke, as it seemed to me, and broke off a love affair. I took a job, lived alone, went on writing, fell in love. I was young, full of energy, and the book seemed to mean that others agreed I was a poet. Because I was also determined to have a "full" woman's life, I plunged in my early twenties into marriage and had three children before I was thirty. There was nothing overt in the environment to warn me: these were the fifties, and in reaction to the earlier wave of feminism, middle-class women were making careers of domestic perfection, working to send their husbands through professional schools, then retiring to raise large families. People were moving out to the suburbs, technology was going to be the answer to everything, even sex; the family was in its glory. Life was extremely private; women were isolated from each other by the loyalties of marriage. I have a sense that women didn't talk to each other much in the fifties—not about their secret emptinesses, their frustrations. I went on trying to write; my second book and first child appeared in the same month. But by the time that book came out I was already dissatisfied with those poems, which seemed to me mere exercises for poems I hadn't written. The book was praised, however, for its "gracefulness"; I had a marriage and a child. If there were doubts, if there were periods of null depression or active despairing, these could only mean that I was ungrateful, insatiable, perhaps a monster.

About the time my third child was born, I felt that I had either to consider myself a failed woman and a failed poet, or to try to find some synthesis by which to understand what was happening to me. What frightened me most was the sense of drift, of being pulled along on a current which called itself my destiny, but in which I seemed to be losing touch with whoever I had been, with the girl who had experienced her own will and energy almost ecstatically at times, walking around a city or riding a train at night or typing in a student room. In a poem about my grandmother I wrote (of myself): "A young girl, thought sleeping, is certified dead." [5] I was writing very little, partly from fatigue, that female fatigue of suppressed anger and the loss of contact with her own being; partly from the discontinuity of female life with its attention to small chores, errands, work that others constantly undo, small children's constant needs. What I did write was unconvincing to me; my anger and frustration were hard to acknowledge in or out of poems because in fact I cared a great deal about my husband and my children. Trying to look back and understand that time I have tried to analyze the real nature of the conflict. Most, if not all, human lives

5. "Halfway," in *Necessities of Life* [*Rich's note*].

are full of fantasy—passive day-dreaming which need not be acted on. But to write poetry or fiction, or even to think well, is not to fantasize, or to put fantasies on paper. For a poem to coalesce, for a character or an action to take shape, there has to be an imaginative transformation of reality which is in no way passive. And a certain freedom of the mind is needed—freedom to press on, to enter the currents of your thought like a glider pilot, knowing that your motion can be sustained, that the buoyancy of your attention will not be suddenly snatched away. Moreover, if the imagination is to transcend and transform experience it has to question, to challenge, to conceive of alternatives, perhaps to the very life you are living at that moment. You have to be free to play around with the notion that day might be night, love might be hate; nothing can be too sacred for the imagination to turn into its opposite or to call experimentally by another name. For writing is re-naming. Now, to be maternally with small children all day in the old way, to be with a man in the old way of marriage, requires a holding-back, a putting-aside of that imaginative activity, and seems to demand instead a kind of conservatism. I want to make it clear that I am *not* saying that in order to write well, or think well, it is necessary to become unavailable to others, or to become a devouring ego. This has been the myth of the masculine artist and thinker; and I repeat, I do not accept it. But to be a female human being trying to fulfill traditional female functions in a traditional way *is* in direct conflict with the subversive function of the imagination. The word traditional is important here. There must be ways, and we will be finding out more and more about them, in which the energy of creation and the energy of relation can be united. But in those earlier years I always felt the conflict as a failure of love in myself. I had thought I was choosing a full life: the life available to most men, in which sexuality, work, and parenthood could coexist. But I felt, at 29, guilt toward the people closest to me, and guilty toward my own being.

I wanted, then, more than anything, the one thing of which there was never enough: time to think, time to write. The fifties and early sixties were years of rapid revelations: the sit-ins and marches in the South, the Bay of Pigs, the early anti-war movement, raised large questions—questions for which the masculine world of the academy around me seemed to have expert and fluent answers. But I needed desperately to think for myself—about pacifism and dissent and violence, about poetry and society and about my own relationship to all these things. For about ten years I was reading in fierce snatches, scribbling in notebooks, writing poetry in fragments; I was looking desperately for clues, because if there were no clues then I thought I might be insane. I wrote in a notebook about this time:

Paralyzed by the sense that there exists a mesh of relationships—

e.g. between my anger at the children, my sensual life, pacifism, sex, (I mean sex in its broadest significance, not merely sexual desire)—an interconnectedness which, if I could see it, make it valid, would give me back myself, make it possible to function lucidly and passionately. Yet I grope in and out among these dark webs.

I think I began at this point to feel that politics was not something "out there" but something "in here" and of the essence of my condition.

In the late fifties I was able to write, for the first time, directly about experiencing myself as a woman. The poem was jotted in fragments during children's naps, brief hours in a library, or at 3 a.m. after rising with a wakeful child. I despaired of doing any continuous work at this time. Yet I began to feel that my fragments and scraps had a common consciousness and a common theme, one which I would have been very unwilling to put on paper at an earlier time because I had been taught that poetry should be "universal," which meant, of course, non-female. Until then I had tried very much *not* to identify myself as a female poet. Over two years I wrote a 10-part poem called "Snapshots of a Daughter-in-Law," [6] in a longer, looser mode than I'd ever trusted myself with before. It was an extraordinary relief to write that poem. It strikes me now as too literary, too dependent on allusion; I hadn't found the courage yet to do without authorities, or even to use the pronoun "I"—the woman in the poem is always "she." One section of it, No. 2, concerns a woman who thinks she is going mad; she is haunted by voices telling her to resist and rebel, voices which she can hear but not obey.

The poem "Orion," [7] written five years later, is a poem of reconnection with a part of myself I had felt I was losing—the active principle, the energetic imagination, the "half-brother" whom I projected, as I had for many years, into the constellation Orion. It's no accident that the words "cold and egotistical" appear in this poem, and are applied to myself. The choice still seemed to be between "love"—womanly, maternal love, altruistic love—a love defined and ruled by the weight of an entire culture; and egotism—a force directed by men into creation, achievement, ambition, often at the expense of others, but justifiably so. For weren't they men, and wasn't that their destiny as womanly love was ours? I know now that the alternatives are false ones—that the word "love" is itself in need of re-vision.

There is a companion poem to "Orion," written three years later, in which at last the woman in the poem and the woman writing the

6. See p. 12, above.
7. See p. 35, above.

poem become the same person. It is called "Planetarium," [8] and it was written after a visit to a real planetarium, where I read an account of the work of Caroline Herschel, the astronomer, who worked with her brother William, but whose name remained obscure, as his did not.

In closing I want to tell you about a dream I had last summer. I dreamed I was asked to read my poetry at a mass women's meeting, but when I began to read, what came out were the lyrics of a blues song. I share this dream with you because it seemed to me to say a lot about the problems and the future of the woman writer, and probably of women in general. The awakening of consciousness is not like the crossing of a frontier—one step, and you are in another country. Much of woman's poetry has been of the nature of the blues song: a cry of pain, of victimization, or a lyric of seduction. And today, much poetry by women—and prose for that matter—is charged with anger. I think we need to go through that anger, and we will betray our own reality if we try, as Virginia Woolf was trying, for an objectivity, a detachment, that would make us sound more like Jane Austen or Shakespeare. We know more than Jane Austen or Shakespeare knew: more than Jane Austen because our lives are more complex, more than Shakespeare because we know more about the lives of women, Jane Austen and Virginia Woolf included.

Both the victimization and the anger experienced by women are real, and have real sources, everywhere in the environment, built into society. They must go on being tapped and explored by poets, among others. We can neither deny them, nor can we rest there. They are our birth-pains, and we are bearing ourselves. We would be failing each other as writers and as women, if we neglected or denied what is negative, regressive, or Sisyphean in our inwardness.

We all know that there is another story to be told. I am curious and expectant about the future of the masculine consciousness. I feel in the work of the men whose poetry I read today a deep pessimism and fatalistic grief; and I wonder if it isn't the masculine side of what women have experienced, the price of masculine dominance. One thing I am sure of: just as woman is becoming her own midwife, creating herself anew, so man will have to learn to gestate and give birth to his own subjectivity—something he has frequently wanted woman to do for him. We can go on trying to talk to each other, we can sometimes help each other, poetry and fiction can show us what the other is going through; but women can no longer be primarily mothers and muses for men: we have our own work cut out for us.

8. See p. 45, above.

The Anti-Feminist Woman (1972) †

* * *

Patriarchal organization and culture have been under question for some time, and until recently the best-known questioners have been men. Erich Neumann, a disciple of Jung, wrote in 1952 (in his introduction to *The Great Mother*):

> . . . this problem of the Feminine has equal importance for the psychologist of culture, who realizes that the peril of present-day mankind springs in large part from the one-sidedly patriarchal development of the male intellectual consciousness, which is no longer kept in balance by the matriarchal world of the psyche.

Engels earlier connected the advent of the patriarchal family with the beginnings of property-hunger, slavery, war as acquisitive pillage, and ultimately the State itself with its sanction and encouragement of human exploitation. Engels had, of course, as little regard for religion and mythology as Neumann has interest in the labor theory of value. Neumann is concerned not with the liberation of actual women, or even with the political organization of men, but with the collective loss and fragmentation suffered by human beings in the denial and suppression of the feminine. He is not interested in establishing that any actual historical "matriarchal stage" existed but he insists that it does exist in the human unconscious and that "the health and creativity of every man depend very largely on whether his unconscious can live at peace with this stratum of the unconscious or consumes itself in strife with it."

But the patriarchy has come into question in another way: as the natural order of things. There is a line of speculative inquiry reaching back for over a century that suggests that a matriarchal social order preceded the patriarchal: for example, J. J. Bachofen's *Das Mutterrecht* (1861) and Robert Briffault's *The Mothers*, a three-volume study first published in 1927 and reprinted in an abridged edition in 1969. Bachofen maintained that civilizations such as the pre-Hellenic were not simply matrilineal but were based on "the religious and civic primacy of womanhood" and that many of their scientific and cultural achievements were lost when the matriarchies were crushed, some to be recovered only centuries later.

More recently, in a fascinating though problematical book, *The*

† From *The New York Review of Books,* XIX, 9 (November 30, 1972), 35–40. Reprinted with permission from the *New York Review of Books*. Copyright © 1972 Nyrev, Inc. The seemingly inappropriate title of this essay derives from the fact that its point of departure is a review of an anti-feminist book by a woman: Midge Decter's *The New Chastity and Other Arguments Against Women's Liberation* (1972). The excerpts given here come after the negative review of the book.

First Sex,[1] Elizabeth Gould Davis has attempted to bring together evidence of this primacy—anthropological, archaeological, mythological, historical—and to draw connections which have long been left undrawn, or which if drawn, as by Bachofen and in our century by Mary Beard (*Woman As a Force in History,* 1945), have been largely ignored or dismissed as unhistorical. While Beard was concerned to point out that much has been swept under the rug, Davis tries to assemble evidence that matriarchies existed, that these may have been the "lost" cultures later remembered and mythologized as the Golden Age, and that there was a deliberate effort to obliterate their memory by the patriarchy—as in the case of mother-goddesses who were later transformed into paternalistic and judgmental gods like Yahweh. (Santayana's remark that "there is no God and Mary is his mother" becomes more than a quip in this context.)

Long before Davis, in the 1930s, Otto Rank was writing that Jewish "monotheism appears as the result of a long struggle against foreign gods who still betrayed the earmarks of an earlier mother-goddess";[2] and that "the Torah which guided the nomadic Jews through the desert represented an original female symbol, a relic of the great Asatic Mother-Goddess."[3] Theodor Reik, in his *Pagan Rites in Judaism* (1964), remarks of the Torah that *"She* is considered older than the world and is assigned a cosmic role. . . . Even in this diluted form we recognize the primal female goddess." Rank points out that the Golden Calf itself was not the proverbial symbol of materialism but a mother symbol.

* * *

Davis's book, while it throws out a wide and potentially illuminating spray of sparks, is not, like Beard's, critical of its sources nor does the author attempt to deal with the special problems of controversy within the fields she draws on. What she does provide is the idea of a historical alternative to a society characterized by dominant, aggressive men and passive, victimized, acquiescent women. Even were only half the scholarship she cites accurate, the idea would remain enormously valuable. Davis's book also suggests the necessity for a new and demanding kind of critical scholarship—a searching re-evaluation of the "respectable" sources as well as of neglected ones, undertaken in the light of feminist perceptions.

* * *

1. Elizabeth Gould Davis, *The First Sex* (Putnam's, 1971; Penguin, 1972, paper) [*Rich's note*].
2. Otto Rank, *Beyond Psychology* (Dover, 1958), p. 240 [*Rich's note*].
3. Ibid., p. 240. Cf. Davis, p. 60 [*Rich's note*].

To think as a feminist means trying to think connectedly about, for example, the science of embryology as it may connect with sexuality (what does it mean, for example, that in the fetus male differentiation occurs only after several weeks); [4] about human body-rhythms and their relation to natural cycles (the menses and the lunar month, the connections between woman, darkness, sleep, and death in the male unconscious; the connections of these with male attitudes and political decisions affecting women); about the uses and criteria of psychology (Phyllis Chesler in her recent *Women and Madness* begins to connect male theories of female psychology with the political and social order). It is easy to say that we cannot ever know what is truly male or truly female. There is much we can know. We do know that these principles have been split apart and set in antagonism within each of us by a male-dominated intellectual and political heritage. That is at least a starting point.

I would like to clarify here the way in which I am using the term patriarchy. By it I mean to imply not simply the tracing of descent through the father, which anthropologists seem to agree is a relatively late phenomenon, but any kind of group organization in which males hold dominant power and determine what part females shall and shall not play, and in which capabilities assigned to women are relegated generally to the mystical and aesthetic and excluded from the practical and political realms. (It is characteristic of patriarchal thinking that these realms are regarded as separate and mutually exclusive.) Such group organization has existed so long that almost all written history, theology, psychology, and cultural anthropology are founded on its premises and contribute to its survival. Based as it is on genital difference, its concept of sex is genitally centered; entire zones of the body (and soul) are to be used simply as means to a genital end.

At the core of the patriarchy is the individual family unit with its division of roles, its values of private ownership, monogamous marriage, emotional possessiveness, the "illegitimacy" of a child born outside legal marriage, the unpaid domestic services of the wife, obedience to authority, judgment and punishment for disobedience. Within this family children learn the characters, sexual and otherwise, that they are to assume, in their turn, as adults. The parents are expected to deliver the child up to the educational system, which will carry it further in this acculturation process; the parents reinforce the values of school and discourage the child from rebelling against authority, even the most corrupt, lest he or she fail to enter the mainstream of the society.

---

4. Mary Jane Sherfey, *The Nature and Evolution of Female Sexuality* (Random House, 1972), pp. 38 and 141 [*Rich's note*].

Throughout, authority derives from a person's status—father, teacher, boss, lawgiver—rather than from his personal qualities. We all know variations on this pattern and most of us can cite instances of unusual mutuality and liberality in families we know or have been part of; but the fact remains that they do not represent the overruling pattern. The sacredness of the family in the patriarchy—sacred in the sense that it is heresy to question its ultimate value—relieves the titular head of it from any real necessity to justify his behavior.

* * *

The patriarchy looks to its women to embody and impersonate the qualities lacking in its institutions—concern for the quality of life, for means rather than for pure goal, a connection with the natural and the extrasensory order. These attributes have been classified as "female" in part because the patriarchy relegates them to women and tends to deny them—with a certain fatalism—to men. The encouragement of such qualities as intuition, sympathy, and access to feeling by a mother in her sons is deplored because this is supposed to make them unfit for the struggle that awaits them in a masculine world. Thus the "masculinity" of that world is perpetuated.

Most early feminists did not question the patriarchal family structure as such. They wanted education, changes in the marriage laws, birth control, suffrage; the struggle to prove that women could be entrusted with such dangerous tools was energy-consuming—and physically dangerous—enough without taking on the patriarchy en bloc. But recently, as a few, mostly white middle-class, women have obtained token "equality" in the form of permission to attend professional schools, to be pediatricians or psychoanalysts or to argue cases in court, their relationship to the patriarchy has become confusing.

When the professor who directs your thesis, the second professor who interviews you for a grant, the editor who hires you for the staff of his magazine, the government official who offers you a position on his committee, the chief surgeon with whom you work as an anesthesiologist, the reviewer who praises you for "logical thinking," the analyst who approves your method of dealing with patients in training, the members of the law firm in which you are the first woman partner, all are male, it is difficult to be sure when and where your "success" begins to build itself on a series of denials, small enough in themselves, perhaps, yet accruing through the invisible process such things follow into acquiescence in a system of values which distrusts and degrades women.

I am not talking here about the loss of some fragile "feminine" quality jeopardized by excellence in reasoning and analysis, or by the desire to have original ideas. I am talking about the consciousness of self as Other which Simone de Beauvoir has described as that being toward whom man often feels fear, guilt, and hostility, and about whom he weaves his least defensible theories. Few women have grown up without this knowledge, lodged as it may be in some collective unconscious, disguised as it may be under codes of chivalry, domestic sentiment, biological reduction, or as it is revealed in poetry, law, theology, popular songs, or dirty jokes. Such knowledge—so long as women are not pressured into denying it—makes them potentially the deepest of all questioners of the social order created by men, and the most genuinely radical of thinkers.

It goes without saying that for "successful" women, male hostility usually takes forms less physical and literal than it does in the lives of their "unliberated" sisters. In Bangla Desh during the revolution, it has been estimated that 200,000 women were raped by Pakistani soldiers. Many were victims, according to Joyce Goldman in the August, 1972, issue of *Ms.*, of highly organized, almost mechanized gang rape. Some were children as young as eight. The husbands, fathers, brothers, fiancés of these women immediately disowned them, made them outcasts of that allegedly revolutionary new society. Many of these women committed suicide, others gave birth to children whom they later murdered. Every one of these women was raped twice: first physically by the enemy soldier, then psychically by the enemy in her own household. I wonder how many women there are, however free and fortunate they consider themselves, who would not respond to that double jeopardy with intense and painful recognition.

The "liberated" woman encounters male hostility in the form of psychic rape, often masked as psychic or physical seduction. It occurs overtly in the classroom where a male teacher denigrates female intellect; more subtly in the committee where she sits as token woman and where her intelligence is treated with benign neglect; in the magnanimous assumption that she is "not like other women" and for this reason is so desirable a colleague, figurehead, or adornment to the establishment (the pitting of woman against woman, woman against herself). At the same time that she is told about her "specialness" she is expected to be flattered, like all women, by flirtation. She is also expected to be flattered by man's sexual self-hatred and sexual confusion, his avowal that "I can talk to women, but not to men," his romanticizing of his sexual dishonesty: "I can't talk to my wife, but I can talk to you."

When she is not flattered, she is accused of causing his impotence. When she responds with strong feeling to any or all of the above, she is charged with emotionalism, hysteria, frigidity, lack of objectivity. A member of the British women's movement remarked on the BBC:

> One of the consequences of living in a world intellectually domi-
> nated by men . . . is that women try to have opinions which will
> satisfy the approved standards of the world; and in the last analy-
> sis, these are standards imposed on them by men, which, in prac-
> tise, means that our opinions are kept fairly rigorously separated
> from our own lived experience. If a woman today wants to have
> opinions which are truly her own, she has to check them against
> her experience; and often not against her personal experience
> alone, *but against a collective one.*[5]

The token woman may come to believe that her personal solution
has not been bought, but awarded her as a prize for her special
qualities. And indeed she may—indeed, must—have special quali-
ties. But her personal solution has been bought; her "liberation" be-
comes another small confirmation of the patriarchal order and its
principle of division.

The great loss that the "special" woman suffers is her separation
from other women, and thus from herself. As soon as she is lulled
by that blandishment about being different, more intelligent, more
beautiful, more human, more committed to rational thinking, more
humorous, more able to "write like a man," a true daughter of the
father-principle, she loses touch with her own innate strength. Un-
derlying the "successful" antifeminist woman's thought is surely the
illusion that "If I can be a special woman, I can be free"—even
though this freedom requires a masculine approach to social dy-
namics, to competition with others, to the very existence of other
human beings and their needs (which are seen as threatening). She
may let herself become concerned with the "status" of other "spe-
cial" women, while she ignores the women typing in the office or
serving in the cafeteria.

* * *

One of the devastating effects of technological capitalism has been
its numbing of the powers of the imagination—specifically, the
power to envision new human and communal relationships. I am
a feminist because I feel endangered, psychically and physically, by
this society, and because I believe that the women's movement is
saying that we have come to an edge of history when men—in so
far as they are embodiments of the patriarchal idea—have become
dangerous to children and other living things, themselves included;
and that we can no longer afford to keep the female principle—the
mother in all women and the woman in many men—straitened

---

5. Anya Bostock, in the BBC Third Programme, *The Listener, August,* 1972 [*Rich's note*].

within the tight little postindustrial family, or within any male-induced notion of where the female principle is valid and where it is not.

* * *

Three Conversations (1974)

These conversations between Adrienne Rich, Barbara Charlesworth Gelpi, and Albert Gelpi were recorded at the Gelpis' home in Stanford, California, on May 3 and 4, 1974. They agreed that since a formal interview would be artificial among friends, the best procedure would be to set the tape recorder going while they talked. The transcript of the tape was edited by all three. The first conversation turns on the role of violence and anger in women's lives and in the women's movement.

AR: Revolutionary violence. Obviously we're not talking about smashing the dishes, beating one's children. Women have done that for centuries. And we've turned our anger even more often into self-destructiveness. But suppose we were running a women's center, let's say, a drop-in counseling center for women in a neighborhood where some men felt very threatened by this, who at some time charged into this hypothetical storefront, and started doing very violent things. Would the moral thing be for us to let them throw the furniture around and break up the place and beat up the women there? Would we choose to defend ourselves physically? Would we use violence against them? Would we pick up chairs and beat them over the heads? Would we use Karate or Tai Kwon Do? I don't think that's a simple question.

AG: No.

AR: And to say that one is *a priori* nonviolent, and secondly feminist, seems to me like trying to compartmentalize two very different things—and I can't see it that way. I have no predilection for physical violence. It horrifies me; I'm scared of it. But that fact makes me realize that I don't even have a choice about it. To say, "morally I'm against violence" is *not* a moral choice for me; I'm scared by it. My whole socialization as a woman has been against it.

BCG: I wonder if that's true of a lot of people who say they're against violence.

AR: Well, there's the other side of it too. Barbara Deming wrote an article in *Liberation* a few years ago [1] which was one of several things that led me to write "The Phenomenology of Anger." She talked about pacifism and anger, and she said that pacifists were alienating young people on the left by denying their own rage. Paci-

1. Barbara Deming, "On Anger," *Liberation*, XVI, 9 (November 1971), 4–9.

fists are as violent as or more violent than other people. Pacifists are angry people, and here they are coming on like lambs and presenting themselves as people who are innately nonviolent. She says, no wonder the young people are turning away. Because we don't seem real. We're not real—even to ourselves; this is just a lie.

BCG: Well, what does she think is the answer to her own feelings of violence? She still in a way believes that pacifism is the answer, since she thinks that this anger can be transcended.

AR: Well, she does think it can be transcended but she has what to me is a mythic notion of women as the carriers of real nonviolence. So women ought to be discovering alternative responses to violence—such as guerrilla theatre, where you take the rapist and make him understand what it is to be raped, but don't harm him physically. But I feel that psychic violence is violence too, and we all use psychic violence in one way or another. It's not enough to say: "I'm not going to kill anybody, I'm not going to beat up on anybody." In a very "nonviolent" way people can be so psychically damaging to other people that they *are* violent. They are not violent in the sense that Nixon is violent or that the Vietnam War was violent or that the ghetto is violent. It's a different kind of violence, but it's *violence*. Here's an example, something I heard about a man in a college community. A women's group had a seminar on rape. The man had been walking around saying that "all these women need is a good fuck, they really want to be raped and so are obsessed with the subject." So one woman sent him a note and said, "I would like to meet you and discuss the whole question of rape." She had in the meantime gathered the women's group together at the meeting place, and the women all piled on this guy and took down his pants and sat on him. They kept telling him, "We're not going to do anything to you. We're not about to take out knives and castrate you, but you're going to find out what it is like to feel powerless." This is what rape is, really; it's feeling totally powerless while someone is acting on you in a totally violent way. I proposed this to Deming and we talked about whether or not that could really drive a guy crazy. Some men are so afraid of castration and so afraid of women that they could just freak out totally. Is that a legitimate answer to rape? Or is that violence too? I mean, the questions get very hairy.

BCG: That seems to me violence.

AR: It's violence; but it seems to me also a legitimate way of dealing with a guy who is going around shooting off his mouth about how he would like to rape women.

BCG: It's certainly a reasonable tactic. What did Barbara Deming think?

AR: Well, she was saying that we should find alternate methods, guerrilla theatre methods of demonstrating what has been done to us so that men will understand. She does believe that we can get men to understand and change what they are doing to women. I'm less certain of that. I'm certain of it in the long run, but I'm not certain of it in short-run ways. I mean, a lot of men—I'm not saying all men, but many men—are misogynists, and are threatened by and hate women. I don't think it's going to be that easy to demonstrate to them what they're doing. Because they need to do that. It's a psychic need, a disease. The dread and hatred of women—a lot has been written about that—Horney, H. R. Hays, Neumann. . . .[2]

BCG: As you talk it reminds me of another kind of violent feeling. Mothers' voices in a children's playground—the violence implicit so often in mothers' relationships with their children. The violence that I discovered in myself. I've talked to other mothers too. I thought I had no temper until I had children. The harshness in harassed mothers' voices as they talk to children in the playground. As you talk about the men who are misogynists, I wonder: where does it start? You get the frustrated women, who then bring up their children in anger, all of them grating against each other. And it's all so sad. You just wonder if there's something to do about that violence. Again, if only that could be expressed; but do we bring guerrilla theatre into the playground? It's there, of course, among the children.

AR: Of course. But you know raising a child in this society is such a lonely task, no matter how middle-class you are or what resources you have. Finally, all the moral responsibility is on the mother. However heavy a figure the father is in Freud, it's the mother who's seen as the destructive one, the purveyor of evil. The guilt of mothers is so intense. It's built-in with our system, and it's partly because there's the one woman who is responsible for those children. No matter how good a father is and no matter how many babysitter surrogates there are, you still end up feeling that if your children stammer or their noses run or they walk funny, it's because of you and nobody else. And if they're successful or beautiful or whatever, it's just because you have barely been able to achieve that. If there were more people truly responsible for every child, I think there would be less anger, there would be less violence. Children wouldn't be so angry at their mothers. What really has been striking me lately—since I have been able to detach myself from the mother scene—is that American children are angry, frustrated people for the most part. Kids are unhappy in this society. I think

2. Cf., e.g., Karen Horney, "The Dread of Women," *International Journal of Psychoanalysis*, XIII (1932), 348 ff.; H. R. Hays, *The Dangerous Sex* (New York: Putnam Sons, 1964); Erich Neumann, "The Psychological Stages of Feminine Development," translated and revised by Hildegard Nagel and Jane Pratt, *Spring* (journal of the Analytical Psychology Club), 1959.

it's partly because they don't have other adults to relate to, and they are supposed to relate with such intensity to the mother. But a lot of the time the mother has other things she wants and needs to do, she can't be that polar figure or lightning rod, to take everything that comes down on her and deflect it.

BCG: Yes—certainly my own feeling is that children are communal creatures. Children love communality, they really do; they thrive.

AR: Absolutely; given the chance they'll take it. That's what they want, not in fact, to be attached to one woman who is sitting at home all day gritting her teeth. Yet in middle-class America that's what we've been led to think is the best thing for them. And an upwardly mobile woman will tend to accept that too. That's how the whole structure is set up. I don't know if you've run into this, but I did and a lot of women I know did: school schedules are set up on the premise that there is a mama at home who has nothing to do but wait for the kids; so lunch hour is shifted from one semester to the next, or coming-home time is shifted. What else has she to do except clean the fishbowl and water the plants and wait for the lunch hour when the children come home? And that is an incredible lie because the majority of women in this country work outside the home, whether they have to or choose to.

BCG: Yes, they're made to feel guilty for that—the very fact that they have to work is an added guilt.

AR: Whether they have to or choose to. The myth of the full-time mother against the realities of women's lives. Even at that poetry conference last week at Berkeley, there was no child-care, let alone the fact that the charge was twenty-five dollars for the weekend. And the reason I met later with the Berkeley women students is that they called me and said a lot of the women couldn't come to the conference because (a) they couldn't get away because they had kids, and (b) they couldn't afford twenty-five dollars. They're graduate students. A few had brought children and felt they had to leave when the kids got restless. If a woman can work it out and improvise, it's okay, but if she can't it's her fault, she's guilty and a failure and she can't go where she wants to go. No wonder mothers get angry with their children. It's hard to get angry at the patriarchy, which is an abstraction. It's much easier to get angry at one small child screaming at you. You hit out either at another woman or at a child; you never hit at the man.

BCG: Of course mothers are now realizing more that they're just getting angry at the closest object.

AR: I saw a documentary film called *Janey's Janey*, about a woman on welfare, a working-class woman, married to a working-class man. She acknowledges that his life was tough. He came home from the factory every day and beat up on her. She understood why, but she finally decided she wasn't going to take this anymore, and she threw him out. Now she has four kids, she's on welfare, and the film just follows her around her life. And she talks about the violence that comes down from the working-class man to the working-class woman and from her onto the kids. When she saw this as the inevitable pattern, she decided finally that she had to get rid of it.

BCG: Does she find now that she doesn't have the same feelings of violence towards her children?

AR: Well, she doesn't say that, but she talks about the fact that now she is getting together with other women—first in the PTA, then with the welfare mothers—and that they're discovering that they can organize themselves. When they organize themselves there's some action, and instead of committing violence on your children you channel the anger into the outer world, you start dealing with that world. She said, wonderfully, when you've got nothing you can't imagine that you could have anything. But once you get a little, you begin to realize you can have a lot. She's really talking about rising expectations: "We want a different kind of school for our children. We want a new kind of welfare system. We're going to get it; we're going to have it. But when we were ignorant of the possibilities we didn't think we could have aything."

BCG: Even to know what you want. It is also, of course, a channeling of violence. I think it's why Bobby Seale [3] has turned against indiscriminate violence. It becomes possible that you can even define what you are. That definition is itself wonderfully releasing.

AR: The most self-destructive violence is committed by people who don't know *what* they want, who only know that they are in a state of horrible need, horrible frustration. If a woman really knows what she wants, she's going to tell her husband: "Look, these are my needs." Or she's going to leave him, or look for a job, or speak up to her boss. She's not going to go on doing it to her kids or herself. But women's needs have been defined for us by men and we've often felt we were monstrous or crazy when we tried to assert ourselves. I really know how it feels—that obscure, boiling anger.

BCG: Yes, it was a horrible revelation—terrible to have the feelings of violence, but then worse to give expression to them. There can be all kinds of explanations, but as a mother suddenly I found myself a child again.

3. With Huey Newton, Bobby Seale founded the Black Panther Party; they are the leaders and theoreticians of the Party.

AR: I felt that too. I know just what you mean. But say something more about that. How you felt like a child.

BCG: I don't know—the old pain and the old frustration—

AR: An ignorance of what it was that was hurting you?

BCG: It was as if all the years in between had dropped away and I was coping with—oh, say if I entered into children's quarrels—I was reacting as a child would. I hated along with the children. And all the way through I was reading books on child psychology, which were all saying you should get on top of it.

AR: And also, all of which assume that there is a totally unconflicted mother there twenty-four hours a day. A totally unconflicted woman—that's the thing that's posited in all those books. Surely feeling like a child is a way of saying we felt powerless. I know it had to do for me with a world in which men acted and lived and which I felt was denying me my existence. As I was saying, you can't get angry at the patriarchy, not in that way. You're alone with that kid, so you turn on him because he's turned the table over and dropped all the water color paints on the floor or something. But think of a world in which it is assumed that if you're a couple both people work part-time, so that public and private life are not separated out that way; child care is part of what everybody does and working in the outer world is part of what everybody does. It doesn't matter what your gender is, you do both. Male and female both take on the housekeeping and child care. Those are the great unpaid services that women now render to the economy. Without women doing that unpaid, for love, the economy would not exist, it would crumble. But in a society where it was assumed that both female and male would care for children, and would also do other things, it would not be so necessary for a woman or a man to achieve in a sterile way. If we accord such immense importance to the private and emotional zones, and say that here is finally where values come from, humanistic or otherwise, then we should want this zone to be modulated by *both* women and men. Women would cease being the makers of refuge for men and children. Then you would have a wholly different kind of structure. Now we're laboring under a structure that's evolved out of thinking about women and men as dividing up the realms separately with no crossing over. Woman is privacy, home, domesticity, emotional refuge, subjectivity. Man is achievement, aggression, outer world, economics, etc.

But back to child care and back to motherhood. Violence and motherhood—that fascinates me. Is there something finally that almost intrinsically connects them? The recurrent myth of the destructive mother, the evil mother, etc. Or is the violence something that has come out of the nature of the woman-child relationship in a patriarchy? If a woman felt that she had real power, that her existence had a meaning beyond motherhood, that she could alter reality, would she still feel the kind of destructive anger, self-hatred, that leads to mother-child violence? Or does mother-child violence come out of her inability to express anger against men because she knows that they are the people who have the real power? You rarely, except in an extreme situation, express and act on anger against the people who are in control of things, because it's too dangerous; you can't do that.

AG: How do you answer that question? Is violence a psychological factor inherent in the person and therefore in any relationship, or is it a matter of environment?

AR: I think anger is culturally and psychically part of every human being. The question is how do you use anger for change? I don't think anger is negative in and of itself. It gets used in negative ways. But, for example, let's say that I feel anger at you but instead of expressing it to you I go around feeling deeply depressed. I feel so much guilt toward you or respect for you—or fear of your power—that I cannot deal with the fact that I'm angry at you, and so I turn it in on myself. That's a terrible use of anger. If I could say to you, "Look, Al, what you're doing really enrages me, and this is why," we might be able to work through that, in a personal relationship, and transcend the anger finally—and the anger would be very creative.

BCG: Blake said it. Blake's "Poison Tree."

AR: "I was angry with my friend—I told my wrath, my wrath did end." Exactly.

BCG: But "The Poison Tree" says that if you don't, then it becomes terribly destructive.

AR: But, you know, that's crucial because for women to dissemble anger has been a means of survival, and therefore we turn our anger inward. Women's survival and self-respect have been so terribly dependent on male approval. I almost think that we have a history of centuries of women in depression: really angry women, who could have been using their anger creatively, as men have used their anger creatively. I think an enormous amount of male art is anger converted into creation. And women have not often been in a position to do that. And therefore it's not only that there are unwritten books, but many of the books that were written are subdued, they're like banked fires—they're not what they might have been.

BCG: *Wuthering Heights* shows how a woman can use anger creatively and express that anger in a work of art.

AR: Oh, definitely, yes. And so are passages in *Jane Eyre* and *Villette*—it's incredible. I think anger can be a kind of genius if it's acted on.

BCG: But Emily Brontë has both, because after all she writes *Wuthering Heights* but then, when *Wuthering Heights* is badly received. . . .

AR: She's a suicide in a sense; she dies of consumption. Tuberculosis was rampant in England at that time because of health conditions, but it was also a psychosomatic disease; it always has been.

AG: But to the extent that violence depends on external circumstances, those things can be changed so that anger could be used differently or expressed differently.

AR: There was one interesting thing in Marie Louise Von Franz: [4] that in the early period of Nazism in Germany she was analyzing a lot of patients who were solid citizens and would come to her and say, "I feel I must be abnormal, but I cannot agree with the Nazi party. I must be a really weird person." If you deviate from a situation which is described to you as normal, you start feeling abnormal. I'm thinking about all the women who have seen themselves as psychotic and have acted psychotically, indeed, acted it out, because they could not accept the situation, which is new in history—not a traditional role: namely, the situation of the American middle-class woman who is expected to spend her life full-time on child care.

The second conversation grew out of discussing the fact that we are attracted to poets who articulate images drawn from their unconscious and speaking to our unconscious, and the fact that women can find something for themselves in the poetry of men like Shelley and Lawrence because, while these poets are sexist, their imaginations act from their "feminine," intuitive nature.

AR: What in the past did we go to poetry for—I'm speaking now as a woman—specifically what did we go to men's poetry for? Or even to women's poetry? Wasn't it for those unconscious perceptions, if anything, that seemed to be speaking to something in our own unconscious? Now that thing in our own unconscious has become more conscious. We are aware of a lot of hungers and longings and denials and frustrations that we were only unconsciously aware of in the past. What does this do to the way we now read the poetry of the past, especially by men—since that is the major tradition? And how is it going to affect the way we read poetry written in the future? Many women are saying that much of this art has never really talked about us in our deepest mode of being, in our nonobjectified mode of being, our own mode of being as opposed to what we had laid on us. The great silence in poems about lesbians and all women who are not defined by the men in their lives. Which is one reason why women's poetry is important to women now.

4. A Jungian psychologist.

BCG: Do you think there are dangers in becoming too conscious? If you start consciously trying to come to these perceptions, are the perceptions going to change into dogmas, party slogans?

AR: Well, I still believe that the energy of poetry comes from the unconscious and always will. So a poetry which could affirm woman or the female, which could affirm a bisexual vision, or which could affirm a whole other way of being male and female as part of its consciousness, as part of its tradition, such a poetry of the future would still, it seems to me, be churning up new unconscious material, which we would be fascinated and influenced by. If it's not doing that, then it's not poetry as far as I'm concerned. Then it is slogans and pamphlets, which are valuable—those things can be useful—but it's not poetry.

BCG: You're thinking that the slogans and pamphlets can then finally affect the unconscious so that the images that would come from the unconscious and thereby revivify and renew the world would be reacting to a greater conscious understanding of male-female relationships, of what the feminine really is. Is that what you're thinking?

AG: Not only that, but the range of perceptions and responses that the unconscious might churn up or tap could be broadened if we acknowledged the bisexual nature of the psyche. Then instead of thinking of the unconscious as tapping the female aspects of the psyche or the masculine, there would be a much broader range of possibilities and responses.

BCG: Al didn't hear, I think, what you were saying about the woman who had come to new understandings of light.

AR: This is a woman I met at a conference in Boston. It was about poetry, but we got to talking about Jungian archetypes and so on. Some people were objecting to the whole Jungian thing as perpetuating sexist stereotypes, and she was saying she didn't feel trapped in it. She had for years had very archetypal dreams and for a long time when the sun had appeared to her in the dreams, it felt like a masculine presence. Recently with a different kind of consciousness about what it was to be female, she'd been having dreams in which the sun and light appeared as female and maternal presences, not as patriarchal archetypes. She felt that our dreams are changing and I guess she would say that the collective unconscious is changing, at least for women, and for some men, so that presumably the images in poetry would be changing.

AG: The collective unconscious anyway has to be mediated through the individual psyche. But that really raises a question I've wanted to ask you for a long time. One of the things that you insist on in your poetry is both a psychological and a political dimension and on making the connection between the psychological and the political. But that seems to me uncharacteristic of most politically active people, especially radicals.

AR: It's not uncharacteristic, though, of feminists. I think that feminism is the place where in the most natural, organic way subjectivity and politics have to come together. For instance, Phyllis Chesler's book.[5] It's not a very political book, but it does try to attack the ways in which women are labeled as crazy to prevent them from having access to their own powers. The mental asylum as a prison for women. Even on that level, the psychological becomes political. More lobotomies and more electro-shock therapy and more psycho-surgery are performed on women than on men by far; the margin is incredible. So madness, i.e., eruptions, disturbances of the unconscious, have had a very political meaning for women all along.

AG: But it seems to me that the response of a lot of feminists would be to say: since we're really threatened politically in society, we can't get distracted into talking about subjective psychological factors; we've got to go out and change conditions.

AR: I think you're really talking about women who are, quite correctly, but narrowly, into equal pay for equal work, more women's appointments, and so on. Academic and professional women often have had to deny their own subjectivity in order to survive in the patriarchy. They have learned to play the game like a man and seek power on male terms. If they are trying to get more power for other women, that's fine. But I don't see a radical feminism as proceeding from anything but a connection between inner and outer. We are attempting, in fact, to break down that fragmentation of inner and outer in every possible realm. The psyche and the world out there are being acted on and interacting intensely all the time. There is no such thing as the private psyche, whether you're a woman—or a man, for that matter. Nor do I see anything but reformism in a politics that denies the unconscious life and the need for transcendence. A lot of women, both in and out of universities, are trying to think about what it means to be female in and of itself, outside of stereotypes and roles, and about the potential of femaleness as a positive value. And about the reversals that have been practiced on women so that it becomes hard to think about ourselves at all. Mary Daly's [6] very good on that: patriarchy calls something by a pejorative name, and you start thinking of it as a negative value. It may be a positive strength to you as a woman, but it's always been named pejoratively. A nice example:

5. Phyllis Chesler. *Women and Madness* (New York: Doubleday, 1972); reviewed by Adrienne Rich in the *New York Times Book Review*, December 31, 1972, pp. 1, 20–21.
6. Mary Daly. *Beyond God the Father: Toward a Philosophy of Women's Liberation* (Boston: Beacon Press, 1973); reviewed by Adrienne Rich in the *Washington Post Book World* (November 11, 1973), pp. 2–3.

there is an article in *Women, Culture, and Society* [7] about the so-called "weak ego boundaries" of women—which might be a negative way of describing the fact that women have tremendous powers of intuitive identification and sympathy with other people. And, yes, a woman could get totally lost in that—she can lose all sense of her own ego, but that is not necessary—it might be a source of power.

BCG: John Keats had weak ego boundaries.

AR: Negative capability. Exactly. Any artist has to have it to some extent.

BCG: Well, again, Jung thinks weak ego boundaries are absolutely necessary.

AR: The male ego, which is described as the strong ego, could really be the weak ego, because it encapsulates itself and will not let itself be threatened or vulnerable to other people.

BCG: And becomes then destructive.

AR: What I really love in Daly is her constant insistence that the people who name things have the power and that everything has been named by men, and the questions have been framed by men, and so women's questions are nonquestions. Given that, you have to be constantly critiquing even the tools that you use to explore and define what it is to be female.

BCG: I wanted to bring you back to poetry. Are you thinking: what good does it do women to have poets writing poems about how great women are, since the really great thing is to write poems?

AR: Well, that's going even further than I was going, but *yes!* In fact, that was something I was toying around with in that poem "The Demon Lover," although I hadn't really zeroed in on it. That question was very much afflicting me at the time: do you, as a woman poet, really want to be Ronsard writing the sonnet to Hélène, or do you want to be Hélène, immortalized so that when she's old and gray and nodding by the fire, they'll point to her and say, that's the woman Ronsard sang about? But again, you put it very neatly, what good does it do to be the woman that the poems are written about, and beyond that, what good does it do women to have these poems about women exist? Poems in which women are all beautiful, and preferably asleep. Of course, others are full of unconscious material which says that the female principle is the source of life, of power, of energy, etc., etc., etc. You can really wire into that kind of poem as a woman, but you don't quite know why. You feel very attracted to it; it does something for you, more than those sonnets about how beautiful or unaccommodating some woman is. But what difference, finally, has it made in women's lives

7. Nancy Chodorow, "Family Structure and Feminine Personality," in *Women, Culture, and Society,* ed. Michelle Zim- balist Rosaldo and Louise Lamphere (Stanford, Calif.: Stanford University Press, 1974), pp. 43–66.

that those poems existed? When I read "The Idea of Order at Key West" for the first time, I really felt wired into that poem because it's about a woman whose singing was establishing the order of things—the order of the universe. I identified with her, not the men in the poem.

AG: But it's in Wallace Stevens' mind.

AR: Yes. If a woman had written that poem, my God!

AG: But it seems to me we're coming back to the same question. I thought you were making a political statement saying that poems can't be validated unless they are changing the conditions which keep women in servitude or relative servitude. Then I thought Barbara was translating that political statement into a psychological statement about women writing the poems.

AR: Certainly when women are not in a state of utter servitude —one of the things we do is write poems. We do a lot of other things, but one of the things we do is write poems. I am made uneasy by the notion that one would dictate *a priori* what kind of poetry should be written. But what I am asking myself is not, if we had a political program what kind of poems would poets be taught to write, but if we were in an altered state of consciousness, if we were free of the dreck of the past, of the stereotypes, of the projections, of all the ways in which women have been used as esthetic objects, what kind of poetry would we have then? It's not like wanting to lay out a program and saying that this is what we should have and this is what poets had better be writing about. I really want to dream about what poems could be written in the future.

BCG: Shelley wrote about Intellectual Beauty as woman, and yet he used his women. . . .

AR: Yes, and suppose we no longer had that split even, because I cannot think of a single male poet, however marvelously he has written about the female principle or intellectual beauty, who hasn't misused and abused actual women. It's just appallingly true. I am saying that politically and psychically and in every way it would be better if artists had their work and their lives integrated. I would want to try to do that for myself. I think that a lot of women are trying to do that. That doesn't mean that there wouldn't be a lot of unconscious images coming up in your work. But consciously you try to integrate as much as possible. I think it would make a difference in the world.

AG: Sure. But I would think that a woman poet would write some poems for the short run—it may not be so short—to shock people into recognizing and changing external social and political conditions. And there would be other kinds of poems you might write which draw on the unconscious and on psychological resources, the anxieties and myths which would carry you really further into the possibility of the future. And I was wondering whether those two impulses are consonant in the writing of the poems you've been writing in the last few years.

AR: I think that we acknowledge that there are different kinds of poems, that in one's complex life there are moments when you use certain types of poems and other moments when you use other kinds of poems. Some fairly uncomplicated poems hit you at a certain point, when that is exactly what you need. They can make an immense psychic difference—open windows of consciousness— yet lack a certain kind of density. Maybe the poetry that you go on reading over and over all your life, geting more and more out of it, would be a much more complex, dense kind of poetry. But I think there's room for both. Also, a lot of women are now writing poems out of their experience, who have never written poetry before. What might sound like something very simplistic and propagandistic in a poem by such a woman, for *her* might represent a very radical, dangerous exploration. And that's important, too; I'm not about to write that off. I think that it's too easy to see that kind of poem in the context of the whole long complicated male tradition with its baroque, in-group quality and not realize that that woman might have gone out on a limb and taken a risk every bit as painful as D. H. Lawrence was taking when he wrote as a man out of a consciousness that was very radical for his time and place. One honors the risk, maybe. And it can speak to others who are taking it.

AG: What you say makes sense; what I might read as sloganizing in a poem may be a very deep thrust.

AR: I still think you can say that something is a good poem or not. That's different, because there are so many things that happen in a good poem. There's sound and rhythm and language being used in an original way. And finally, I would think that a really good poem opens up a possibility for other poems, rather than being the end of a succession of things. Instead of wrapping something up it explodes the possibilities.

The third conversation took off from a speculative question about the political vision motivating the women's movement.

AG: What kind of society do you envision at the end of the travail and conflict and anxiety all around us?

AR: Certainly a society where we could experience our deepest needs and our deepest requirements for survival as sanity rather than insanity. So often when women are in touch with our best instincts, we feel we're crazy. In patriarchal terms, we're a little off the edge. A society where one need not apologize for whatever form one wants for one's life—whether the family in a traditional sense, or homosexuality, or something else. A society where one simply need not spend so much energy constructing a viable existence, where mere survival would not take such a toll.

BCG: I know exactly what you mean. Feminism finally should allow each person to move—man or woman. Each person should be allowed room; there would be no programming for communities or for nuclear families or. . . .

AR: A very much more diversified society than any revolutionary society that we now know, and that includes Cuba, China, or whatever. We were talking earlier about how amazing it is that in Cuba things are provided free which many people here have to struggle for: day-care, education for children, medicine, telephones, public transportation, vacations. But Cuba is also a very sexist and heterosexist society, and when you take that weight of survival off, you still haven't taken off the weight of feeling oppressed as a woman or as a deviant or as somebody who doesn't fit the male-created stereotypes. I really am a socialist, and I think of feminism as inextricable from socialism. But not with socialism put first and then after the revolution attending to the needs of women. I want to put the needs of women first. Start from there rather than from the other place. Because sexism, misogyny, patriarchy is where it all begins.

BCG: And it's very interesting that feminism and socialism have gone together historically. If you start to try to fulfill the needs of women, you almost inevitably become a socialist; there's no other way.

AR: I really do believe that women, when they're free to do so, care more about the environment that they live in, for whatever reasons, than men do. Houses or landscapes or cities—I like to think that if women were in charge of cities they would be much more habitable places. We'd build a city thinking about how people are going to connect with each other rather than about how power is going to be represented in huge buildings and skyscrapers and how money is going to pass from hand to hand.

Women's gift for relationship is fundamental, I think. We can say it's been socialized into us, but I also think that for women there isn't that radical split between self and others, because what was within us comes out of us and we still love it and care for it and we still relate to it. It's still part of us in some way. I'm not antibiological by a long shot in my thinking. I want to reinterpret biology and use it differently. I'm perfectly willing to say there is something about the fact that women have borne life that is important. But don't let it be used the way it's been used against us, whether mothers or non-mothers.

BCG: The human thrust or the human idea time and again has this notion of allowing each person room. Loving each person as himself, while not taking that person's standard, that person's way of living as necessarily how *you* will be, how *you* live. And that's essential to the humanistic vision. It's always there, and it's always lost.

AR: Yes, it is always lost. That's what I was immediately going to say. It's always there but we don't have it. We never have it. As long as you have a relationship between two sexes in which one sex can tell the other how to be, you are not going to have that vision. It's going to fade and slip through your fingers.

AG: The revolution starts in the psyche, then, and moves out.

AR: No, what I'm saying is that feminism—woman's consciousness—ultimately has to break down that dichotomy. Once you stop splitting inner and outer, you have to stop splitting all those other dichotomies, which I think proceed from that. Yourself-other, head-body, psyche-politics, them-us. The good society would be one in which those divisions would be broken down, and there was much more flow back and forth. But I don't know what that would be like. I absolutely cannot imagine what it would be like to be a woman in a nonpatriarchal society. At moments I have this little glimmer of it. When I'm in a group of women, where I have a sense of real energy flowing and of power in the best sense—not power of domination, but just access to sources—I have some sense of what that could be like. But it's very rare that I can imagine even that. And I am a privileged woman. This is the other thing that really blows my mind. I think of myself as being terribly over-privileged, having extraordinary kinds of freedom for many reasons. Education, class, race, money, privileges of all kinds. And if I'm feeling much of the time as restricted and constricted as I'm feeling, who am one of the more privileged women, a token woman, then I realize that my illusion of freedom is an illusion, and that until all women have access to their potential I can have no real liberation. I have no idea what I, what any of us can have access to in a sexually different kind of world. I think it would be simply incredible.

BCG: Of course, I think that the sense of restriction can be greater just because of the greater consciousness. There are women finally very much more restricted who don't feel themselves restricted, because they are unconscious. . . .

AR: But that is tragic, too. It's not knowing where you are.

BCG: Oh, yes, I'm not saying that it's good, but it's those advantages which have led to greater and greater consciousness, and many women either can't or won't let themselves become aware of their situation.

AR: Letting yourself become aware always means that you have to suffer. It means that you stop accepting your life as given, and that you start thinking about what possibilities there might have been. It's really tough, especially for older women, to think you've spent most of your life in ways that you really hated; a lot of women simply blame themselves and say "It's too late."

BCG: There's also this problem. If you can conceive the possibility of a world in which people would be allowed to *be,* as it were, and yet if women are going to try to bring that world about, they must necessarily oppose men, must start ordering men to be different, whereas the idea behind the whole philosophy of feminism is to let it be. You see what I mean?

AR: Daly talks about the fact that women's presence to each other is experienced by men as an absence. In other words, when women start moving away from some center of the patriarchy, to what Daly calls the boundaries, and start talking to each other, men experience this as an absence to them, whereas women experience it together as a presence. She points out that this space on the boundaries of patriarchy is just as available to men as to women, but men have to choose to move into it. They cannot simply sit in the middle of the patriarchy and say, "Women are turning their backs on us." Because that's not what women are doing. We are turning our faces toward each other. She's also saying, again, that the patriarchy always will name whatever women do as a negation of what it is. They will always say that we are man-hating when we are women-loving women.

BCG: I think of the Christians in the catacombs. It is not trying to take over, to fight by power. It's saying we have another way of thinking about this, another way of acting with each other.

AR: That's my experience of it and I think that's Mary's experience of it. I think there is a kind of masculine projection which sees the women's movement as ultimately ending in guerrilla warfare between men and women. *Kill!* But I think that is a male myth. I still am interested in the question of women and violence, how are women going to protect themselves when men get hysterically violent toward women, as they always have. I do think that there are going to be more and more instances of male violence against women as the women's movement becomes more and more threatening, and that somehow is going to have to be reacted to. I don't think women ought to sit and let themselves be trampled on, but I don't think the women's movement is about killing men. It is about saving the lives of women.

AG: Which men can join in or not.

AR: Yes, right. And maybe save their own lives in the process. But I do see saving the lives of women as a priority. The "humanity" trip—not women's liberation, but human liberation—tends to feel too easy to me. Women have always supported every "human" liberation movement, every movement for social change; there have always been women womaning the barricades, but it's never been for us, or about us. I think that women ought to be putting women first now. Which is not to say that we're against the other half of humanity, but just to say that if we don't put ourselves first, we're never going to make it to full humanity. I think that women ought to be saving women's lives, here and now in 1974.

BCG: Yes, and that involves thinking about other women's lives, and thinking of our lives in relation to other women. Because thinking "*I* have these problems" becomes the old, competitive way, the self-pitying way, the other side of which are anger and hatred and violence.

AG: Also because individual women have saved their own skins in the patriarchy.

AR: By cracking the faces of other women.

BCG: Anyway, I do see that. It offers a kind of vision. . . . What if in the suburbs . . . because feminism is taken as a suburban movement. . . .

AR: It is, except it's not that big in the suburbs, is it really?

BCG: I don't think so; I think that's right.

AR: It's one of the many things said about feminism. You can almost run down a list. Feminism equals suburban middle-class, white women's movement, totally unrelated to the needs of poor blacks, Chicanas. Absolutely untrue. There's a black women's movement, a Chicana movement, there's a new organization of labor union women who say plainly that the male labor movement has *not* answered their needs as women. Another charge: feminism equals man-hating; in other words, all the energy of the women's movement really goes into hating men. I think that's a male myth, a male projection, because in fact for all the anger, real anger that I've heard expressed and have expressed myself about men, it still doesn't amount to what I would think of as man-hating in that kind of cheap sense. It's much more complicated. The anger comes out of a complex sense that many of us are still somehow in relationship to men, whether it is sons or lovers or husbands or whatever, and that the individual man and the patriarchy are two different things and yet they are one. The individual man can always choose to fade into the patriarchy. Whenever he wants to he has that privilege. And no woman has that privilege.

AG: I want to ask one more question. It seems to me that on the one hand you don't want to distinguish between masculine and feminine qualities or tendencies because such a distinction in the patriarchy pegs women in a subservient role, but on the other hand, you see the qualities of the good society as basically feminist and argue that the dichotomies that are the agony of a patriarchal society don't apply to women so immediately.

AR: So am I contradicting myself?

AG: Yes.

AR: Okay. I distinguish between feminine and female and feminist. I think that it's important for me and for women generally right now to be thinking of ourselves as women. We are still laboring under the burden of patriarchal definitions of femininity, of femaleness. So I think attention has got to be paid by women to what it means to be a woman. Just simply. What *we* think it ought to mean, what *we* think it has meant, *our* interpretations replacing patriarchal interpretations. I want to put my energy into that.

Criticism

W. H. AUDEN

Foreword to *A Change of World* †

Reading a poem is an experience analogous to that of encountering a person. Just as one can think and speak separately of a person's physical appearance, his mind, and his character, so one can consider the formal aspects of a poem, its contents, and its spirit while knowing that in the latter case no less than in the former these different aspects are not really separate but an indissoluble trinity-in-unity.

We would rather that our friends were handsome than plain, intelligent than stupid, but in the last analysis it is on account of their character as persons that we accept or reject them. Similarly, in poetry we can put up with a good deal, with poems that are structurally defective, with poems that say nothing particularly new or "amusing," with poems that are a bit crazy; but a poem that is dishonest and pretends to be something other than it is, a poem that is, as it were, so obsessed with itself that it ignores or bellows at or goes on relentlessly boring the reader, we avoid if possible. In art as in life, truthfulness is an absolute essential, good manners of enormous importance.

Every age has its characteristic faults, its typical temptation to overemphasize some virtue at the expense of others, and the typical danger for poets in our age is, perhaps, the desire to be "original." This is natural, for who in his daydreams does not prefer to see himself as a leader rather than a follower, an explorer rather than a cultivator and a settler? Unfortunately, the possibility of realizing such a dream is limited, not only by talent but also by time, and even a superior gift cannot cancel historical priority; he who today climbs the Matterhorn, though he be the greatest climber who ever lived, must tread in Whymper's footsteps.

Radical changes and significant novelty in artistic style can only occur when there has been a radical change in human sensibility to require them. The spectacular events of the present time must not blind us to the fact that we are living not at the beginning but in the middle of a historical epoch; they are not novel but repetitions on a vastly enlarged scale and at a violently accelerated tempo of events which took place long since.

Every poet under fifty-five cherishes, I suspect, a secret grudge against Providence for not getting him born a little earlier. On writing down the obvious names which would occur to everyone as those

† From *A Change of World*, by Adrienne Rich (New Haven: Yale University Press), 1951. Reprinted by permission of the publisher.

of the great figures in "modern" poetry, novels, painting, and music, the innovators, the creators of the new style, I find myself with a list of twenty persons: of these, four were born in the sixties, six in in the seventies, and ten in the eighties. It was these men who were driven to find a new style which could cope with such changes in our civilization as, to mention only four, the collapse of the liberal hope of peaceful change, of revolution through oratory and litera- ture; the dissolution of the traditional community by industrial ur- banization; the exposure of the artist to the styles of every epoch and culture simultaneously; and the skepticism induced by psychol- ogy and anthropology as to the face value of any emotion or belief.

Before a similar crop of revolutionary artists can appear again, there will have to be just such another cultural revolution replacing these attitudes with others. So long as the way in which we regard the world and feel about our existence remains in all essentials the same as that of our predecessors we must follow in their tradition; it would be just as dishonest for us to pretend that their style is in- adequate to our needs as it would have been for them to be content with the style of the Victorians.

Miss Rich, who is, I understand, twenty-one years old, displays a modesty not so common at that age, which disclaims any extraordi- nary vision, and a love for her medium, a determination to ensure that whatever she writes shall, at least, not be shoddily made. In a young poet, as T. S. Eliot has observed, the most promising sign is craftsmanship for it is evidence of a capacity for detachment from the self and its emotions without which no art is possible. Crafts- manship includes, of course, not only a talent for versification but also an ear and an intuitive grasp of much subtler and more diffi- cult matters like proportion, consistency of diction and tone, and the matching of these with the subject at hand; Miss Rich's poems rarely fail on any of these counts.

They make no attempt to conceal their family tree: "A Clock in the Square," for instance, is confessedly related to the poetry of Robert Frost, "Design in Living Colors" to the poetry of Yeats; but what they say is not a parrotlike imitation without understanding but the expression of a genuine personal experience.

The emotions which motivate them—the historical apprehension expressed in "Storm Warnings," the conflict between faith and doubt expressed in "For the Conjunction of Two Planets," the feeling of isolation expressed in "By No Means Native"—are not peculiar to Miss Rich but are among the typical experiences of our time; they are none the less for that uniquely felt by her.

I suggested at the beginning of this introduction that poems are analogous to persons; the poems a reader will encounter in this book are neatly and modestly dressed, speak quietly but do not mumble, respect their elders but are not cowed by them, and do not tell fibs: that, for a first volume, is a good deal.

RANDALL JARRELL

Review of *The Diamond Cutters and Other Poems* †

Adrienne Cecil Rich is an enchanting poet; everybody seems to admit it; and this seems only right. Everybody thinks young things young, Sleeping Beauty beautiful—and the poet whom we see behind the clarity and gravity of Miss Rich's poems cannot help seeming to us a sort of princess in a fairy tale. Her scansion, even, is easy and limpid, close to water, close to air; she lives nearer to perfection (an all-too-easy perfection sometimes—there are a few of Schubert's pieces that are better the first time than they ever are again, and some of Miss Rich's poems are like this) than ordinary poets do, and her imperfections themselves are touching as the awkwardness of anything young and natural is touching. The reader feels that she has only begun to change; thinks, "This young thing, who knows what it may be, old?" Some of her poems are very different from the others, some of her nature is very far from the rest of it, so that one feels that she has room to live in and to grow out into; liking her for what she is is a way of liking her even better for what she may become.

On the third page of "The Diamond Cutters" one comes to "Pictures by Vuillard"; comes to *the wild pear-tree,/ The broken ribbons of the green-and-gold/ Portfolio with sketches form an old/ Algerian campaign; the placid three/ Women at coffee by the window, fates/ Of nothing ominous, waiting for the ring/ Of the postman's bell*. By these, by *the cores of fruit* left on the luncheon-plates, *we are led back where we have never been*, to a world where nothing is tragic, where everything stays at its still, summer-shaded noon. But, asks the poem, what good is this to us, *the destined readers of Stendhal*, who *scarcely think of sighing/ For afternoons that found us born too late? Our prudent envy rarely paces spying/ Under those walls, that lilac-shaded gate./ Yet at this moment, in our private view,/ A breath of common peace, like memory,/ Rustles the branches of the wild pear-tree—/ Air that we should have known, and cannot know.*

† From "New Books in Review," *The Yale Review*, XLVI, 1 (September, 1956), 100–103. Reprinted by permission of Mrs. Randall Jarrell.

This is beautiful enough, individual enough, and truthful enough, loves Vuillard well enough (and oh, that *breath of common peace!* how much of its old power Wordsworth's *common* has kept!), to make a reader unwilling to remark, as he needs to: "Stendhal! *That* perpetually enchanted being, always riding off, young, uniformed, on a spring morning into possibility!" Surely Miss Rich means *destined readers of Sartre and "The Sentimental Education."* This is an awkward crude way of defining the class, just as Miss Rich's way is a glib crude way; the *destined readers,* poor unhappy few, need more of the imagination and devotion that the poet has brought to the Vuillard. (When you call people *we* you find it easy to be unfair to them, since you yourself are included in the condemnation.) When the poet is being a Vuillard-looker she is magical and heartfelt; when she is briefly acting the part of a destined-Stendhal-reader she is rhetorical: *we . . . in monstrous change such consolations find/ As restless mockery sets before the mind/ To deal with what must anger and appall.* Yes, that's in the poem too: when our princess does the meanest chores—and filling out an unfelt portion with reliable rhetoric is a mean one—she sounds for an instant like any Academician. Nor does her "Pictures by Vuillard" contain any intimation of the frozen pictures, exact, photographic, almost academic, that testified during his later years to the boredom and passiveness that had always waited unpainted over at the side of those Victorian rose-windows, small bourgeois paradises, that he half-witnessed, half-created. These are miracles free to us, but that the painter paid for—paid for with part of himself; and when that part was gone the poetry of objects, by the light of common day, became their prose.

Some of Miss Rich's ordinary subjects are the past against the present, museums and their contents, Europe and its contents, youth and middle age, morality. Now and then her reader longs for fewer, or at least odder, morals; reading "O let your human memory end/ Heavy with thought and act./ Claim every joy of paradox/ That time would keep intact" is like getting one of Auden's old carbons for Christmas. But usually her moralizing is part of her own particular life, and usually her influences are a surprise and delight. Think of a young poet, an *intellectual,* who can be influenced by Kipling and Frost! When one reads "Our fathers in their books and speech/ Have made the matter plain:/ The green fields they walked in once/ Will never grow again," one can turn to the very poem, "Our Fathers Also." "The Perennial Answer" is typical neurotic-violent Frost—with one touch of Robert Lowell—and "Autumn Equinox" is almost the best Frost-influenced poem I've ever read. It is the monologue, one leaf-raking afternoon, of an old professor's wife. Once, young, shy, stiff-collared, he had seemed to her "superb in his refusal/ To read aloud from Bryant to the ladies/ Assembled on the boarding-house piazza/ Among the moth-wings of a summer evening." But after some still years of "a life annual, academic," she buys loud curtains, weeps in the moonlight, half-asleep, and answers her husband's "Are you ill, unhappy? Tell me what I can do," with "I'm sick, I guess. I thought that life is different than it is." She sees, but finds no way to change, "the lines of grievous love upon his face." Nothing happens. They "finish off not quite as we began": he reading Dryden's "Satires" by the window, like a mended piece of clockwork, she piling leaves in baskets. Old, patient, staid, calm-sleeping as the dead, they have learned to "wake and take the day for what it is," she has learned to make her terrible minimal complaint about life: "Even autumn/ Can only carry through what spring began."

The girl of "Living in Sin" had not expected that in the studio "morning light/ So coldly would delineate the scraps/ Of last night's cheese and blank sepulchral bottles;/ That on the kitchen shelf among the saucers/ A pair of beetle-eyes would fix her own—/ Envoy from some village in the moldings." This envoy and his fellow, the milkman under whose tread, at dawn, "each separate stair would writhe," are as real as, no more real than, her childhood's "great black bears who seemed more blue than black,/ More violet than blue against the dark—/ Where are you now? upon what track/ Mutter your muffled paws, that used to tread/ So softly, surely, up the creakless stair?" Anticipation and actuality, scenery and whatever it is that living transforms scenery into—the poems feel and express both; and if some part of one wants the poet less ideally normal than she is, the poems more nearly final than they are—for none of them are quite what I have heard Wallace Stevens call "permanent poetry"—one repeats to oneself her "Who sleeps, and dreams, and wakes, and sleeps again/ May dream again." The secondary eloboration of those dreams, her poems, has been so successful that no trace of their original obscurity remains; both the point the poems are making and the way in which they are making it are plain to both reader and writer. Her poetry so thoroughly escapes all of the vices of modernist poetry that it has escaped many of its virtues too. (Beside her, Shakespeare, for instance, seems very complicated and modern and obscure.) She tells us how at Versailles "the cry of closing rings/ For us and for the couples in the wood/ And all good children who are all too good," and begs the children to "be wild today." It seems to me that she herself is, often, a good poet who is all too good—one who can afford to be wild tomorrow; meanwhile, today, she is also an endearing and delightful poet, one who deserves Shakespeare's favorite adjective, *sweet*.

ALBERT GELPI

Adrienne Rich: The Poetics of Change †

The development of a poet's themes, techniques and imagery is an instructive and moving study—if the poet is as compelling as Adrienne Rich is. Her first book was published twenty years ago, and she came into her own in the four collections which constitute her poems since the 'sixties; in sequence, the volumes point the drift of American poetry since the Second World War.

The poems which went into *A Change of World,* selected by W. H. Auden for the Yale Younger Poets Series in 1951, were written in the years just after the War, a period dominated by awesome figures: Eliot, Frost, Stevens, and so on. Poets of the generations after theirs—Auden and Tate, for instance, and later Robert Lowell —seemed to be substantiating Eliot's prediction that poetry should take a turn to a stricter formalism than was needed in the 'teens and 'twenties. Dylan Thomas had been a fascinating exotic; Pound was notorious; Williams represented the only major opposing force, but his influence was small compared to the combined presences of Eliot-Tate-Auden. In fact, American poetry was about to take a turn which would make Williams and Pound the presiding eminences for the new poets; the topography of American poetry looked astonishingly different by the end of the fifties, and even more markedly so by the mid-'sixties. But there was little evidence of the impending shift in 1951 when Adrienne Rich, a Radcliffe senior, made a debut as early as it was auspicious.

In his "Foreword" Auden complimented the "younger poet" somewhat condescendingly for not seeking novelty and instead cultivating the "detachment from the self and its emotions" which makes for craftsmanship, as Eliot had observed. Thus the echoes of Frost, Yeats, Stevens, Robinson, Emily Dickinson and Auden himself in these first poems indicated her intelligence and discretion. Auden sums up the virtues of the poems with the statement that they "are neatly and modestly dressed, speak quietly but do not mumble, respect their elders but are not cowed by them, and do not tell fibs." In other words, the stereotype—prim, fussy, and schoolmarmish— that has corseted and strait-laced women-poets into "poetesses" whom men could deprecate with admiration.

Modest and understated as these poems are, they are—the best of

† From *American Poetry Since 1960,* edited by Robert B. Shaw (Cheadle, Cheshire: Carcanet Press Ltd., 1973), pp. 123–143. Reprinted by permission of the publisher.

them—more interesting than Auden's comments suggest, and the main concerns of the later mature work are adumbrated from the start: the sense of imminent doom in "Storm Warnings", "Eastport to Block Island" and "The Ultimate Act"; the relations between man and woman in "An Unsaid Word" and "Mathilde in Normandy"; the difficulty and necessity of communication in "Stepping Backward"; the metaphysical scepticism of "Air Without Incense" and "For the Conjunction of Two Planets"; the fact of mutability in "A Change of World" and "Walden 1950"; the consequent concentration on the passing moment which almost every one of these pieces exemplifies. Rich's reflex is consistent throughout: she seeks shelter as self-preservation. In "Storm Warnings," the first poem in the book, she prepares against the threats within and without by sealing off a comfortable, weather-proof sanctuary.[1] The only exposure is the keyhole that locks the door. So the finely poised paradoxes of "Afterward" note ruefully that a fond innocence must fall, as it will, to the recognition of limits,[2] Still, acknowledged limits can, *faute de mieux,* raise protective perimeters within which one can learn to operate: not just the walls that enclose the psyche but, by extension, the prosodic and technical conventions that shape the space and time of the poem. Aesthetic form rescues the moment from the flux, as "Designs in Living Colors" says, into a richer and repeated realization; besides, aesthetic form imposes the control that raw emotions demand: "A too-compassionate art is only half an art./ Only such proud restraining purity [as Bach has]/ Restores the else-betrayed, too-human heart" ("At a Bach Concert").

The poems in *A Change of World* display a variety of meters, rhymes and stanzas, and each piece elaborates its convention symmetrically, as in the balance of unresolved dualities in "For the Conjunction of Two Planets". After a while the reader begins to wonder if the artifice, no matter how skillfully wrought, may serve as a partial evasion of the conflicts which are the subject of the poem. The verbal expression may camouflage a refusal to do what "The Ultimate Act" urges: commit that act "beneath a final sun." Limits which are hard to accept may become, in the end, too easy to accept. The precariousness of one's situation makes for the insistence on remaining unattached and unharmed; hence the decorous reserve of the woman toward the man in "An Unsaid Word", "Mathilde in Normandy" and "Stepping Backward". It's "you and I in our accepted frame," and poetry is itself a frame for viewing at a relatively safe distance a changing world divided from and against itself.

The Diamond Cutters (1955) is filled with travel poems, written

1. In the original essay, "Storm Warnings" was quoted in full; in this volume it appears on p. 1.

2. In the original essay, "Afterward" was quoted in full; in this volume it appears on p. 2.

on a Guggenheim in Europe and describing famous places and monuments with the acute eye of the tourist. Even such home scenes as Walden and the Charles River take on the detachment of tourist-views. What makes them more than genteel impressions is the developing metaphor which implies that we are all aliens in a fallen world. The first section of the book is called "Letter from the Land of Sinners": Europe littered with the ruins of time which still conjure up an era of greater beauty and order, perhaps even an arcadia when myths seemed true and we "listened to Primavera speaking flowers." But underneath the nostalgia there is the recognition that the fall into history was so original that Primavera is beyond recall, and we visit the ruins without inhabiting them. In "Ideal Landscape": "The human rose to haunt us everywhere,/ Raw, flawed, and asking more than we could bear." In "The Celebration in the Plaza", after the balloon has popped and the fireworks fizzed out: *"But is that all?* some little children cry./ *All we have left,* their pedagogues reply." At the remains of the "Villa Adriana": "His perfect colonnades at last attain/ The incompleteness of a natural thing."

What then remains? In "Lucifer in the Train" the poet repeats the journey from paradise and proposes, in the accents of Stevens, the old question about the fallen world: "What bird but feeds upon mortality,/ Flies to its young with carrion in its claws?" The unconvincing answer comes in a prayer to Lucifer:

> O foundered angel, first and loneliest
> To turn this bitter sand beneath your hoe,
> Teach us, the newly-landed, what you know;
> After our weary transit, find us rest.

Were rest possible, we could make

> another kind of peace,
> And walk where boughs are green,
> Forgiven by the selves that we have been,
> And learning to forgive. Our apples taste
> Sweeter this year; our gates are falling down,
> And need not be replaced.
> ("Letter from the Land of Sinners")

"Landscape of the Star" draws this secular moral from the quest of the Magi for the Christ-child:

> Our gifts shall bring us home: not to beginnings
> Nor always to the destinations named
> Upon our setting-forth. Our gifts compel,
> Master our ways and lead us in the end
> Where we are most ourselves. . . .

The echoes of Yeats and Stevens and Eliot in all these lines only accentuate the effect of willed conclusion.

For the individual, the dilemma of a "change of world" comes down to the question of "Persons in Time", the title of the second section of *The Diamond Cutters*. Framing this set of narrative and dramatic poems, reminiscent of Frost and the Lowell of *The Mills of the Kavanaghs,* are two reflective pieces. "Concord River" cites Thoreau in an argument for so intense a commitment to the moment that it makes the elements of process into the "absolutes" of a "perfected hour." "The Insomniacs" poses the problem specifically for the artist. Is he merely an actor whose "voice commands the formal stage" to hold off "beyond the wings" "all formless and benighted things / That rhetoric cannot assuage"? The conclusion—and it is merely postulated—points beyond such escapism to postulate an art daring enough

> To live in time, to act in space
> Yet find a ritual to embrace
> Raw towns of man, the pockmarked sun.

However, the later revisions of these lines indicate something of the personal and political commitment which Rich's poetry would, in time, learn to make:

> To live in time, to act in space
> And yet outstare with truthfulness
> New slums of man, the pockmarked sun.

The last section of the volume recapitulates the major concerns: poems (such as "The Snow Queen", "A Walk by the Charles", and "The Tree") in which the individual is the epitome of his mortal and corrupt world; poems (such as "Love in a Museum", "Colophon" and "The Diamond Cutters") which commend the demands of art for forcing the moment to fulfillment in completed form. The poet's continuing attitude toward the submission of experience to the artistic process is revealed in phrases like "distance," "imagination's form so sternly wrought," "incisions in the ice," "tools refined": the hard, cold, clear surface of the engraved and faceted diamond.

Snapshots of a Daughter-in-Law (1963) is the transitional book in Adrienne Rich's development. Eight years had intervened between volumes, and they were years of great change, so that the book begins in one place and ends in another. What happens is the crucial event in the career of any artist: a penetration into experience which makes for a distinguishing style. Her themes—the burden of history, the separateness of individuals, the need for relationship where there is no other transcendence—begin to find their clarifying focus and center: what she is as woman and poet in late-twentieth-century America. The first poems in the book are still quite regular; even so striking a piece as "The Knight" is some-

134 • Albert Gelpi

thing of a tour de force in its proportioned elaboration of a conceit. But by the time the reader encounters the title poem, he knows he is dealing with a sensibility tough, restless, capable of unpredictable leaps and turns:

> Your mind now, mouldering like wedding-cake, . . .
> crumbling to pieces under the knife-edge
> of mere fact. In the prime of your life.
>
> . . . .
>
> A thinking woman sleeps with monsters.
> The beak that grips her, she becomes.
>
> . . . .
>
> The argument *ad feminam,* all the old knives
> that have rusted in my back, I drive in yours,
> *ma semblable, ma soeur!*
>
> . . . .
>
> *Dulce ridens, dulce loquens,*
> she shaves her legs until they gleam
> like petrified mammoth-tusk.

This thinking woman paraphrases Baudelaire, parodies Horace to register the pressures that make the mind moulder. The shock of the imagery is due not merely to its violence (each of the passages refers to a cutting edge) but to an accuracy so unsparing that the imagination reacts psychosomatically: muscles tighten and nerves twinge. The ten sections of "Snapshots" comprise an album of woman as "daughter-in-law," bound into the set of roles which men have established and which female acquiescence has re-enforced. Women-artists—Emily Dickinson, Mary Wollstonecraft, Simone de Beauvoir—stand out as images of resistance and achievement, and they herald the image of fulfillment in the last lines.[3] The self-image projected here is archetypical, at once individual and collective: a signal of forces which would become a national movement within the decade.

Adrienne Rich's earlier poems were praised for their subtlety of rhythm and tone, and these unmetered lines lose none of their subtlety for being more strongly stressed and more freely paced. But in becoming more concrete, her poetry was becoming primarily visual rather than aural, and she has been increasingly successful at imprinting images so indelibly that they convey the meaning without comment or conclusion. The words "eye" and "see" recur insistently (some thirty times) throughout the *Snapshots* volume, and there can be no mistaking her purpose: to "outstare with truthfulness" each moment in the flux of time and thereby live as keenly as

3. In the original essay, "Snapshots of a Daughter-in-Law," section 10, was quoted in full; in this volume it appears on pp. 15–16.

her powers of perception make possible. To be is to see; I am eye. Poetry functions as the vehicle for seeing and for fixing what one comes to see. It is the camera with lens and focus, and poems are snapshots.

Not that art provides a satisfactory alternative to time. Fixing an image dates it, and in the *Snapshots* volume Rich began her custom of dating each poem. The poet outlives the poem, can be dated only on his tombstone; yet each marker points the end. The first section in a sequence called "Readings of History" states her ambivalence about the snapshot-poem by calling the camera "The Evil Eye":

> Your camera stabs me unawares,
> right in my mortal part.
> A womb of celluloid already
> contains my dotage and my total absence.

At the same time the fact of mortality generates the urgency to see: "to know / simply as I know my name / at any given moment, where I stand" ("Double Monologue"); and, with others, to

> spongelike press my gaze
> patiently upon your eyes,
> hold like a photographic plate
> against you my enormous question.
> ("Merely to Know")

To use time redeems it as best we can. Through the cultivation of consciousness we can live through time without merely being its victim. Adrienne Rich recognized the risks and responsibilities; "Prospective Immigrants Please Note" warns the reader of the categorical choice: safe security or a dangerous passage.[4] It is indicative that this poem, written in 1962, comes just at that point in Adrienne Rich's life when Jung says that a person in his thirties, having accomplished his initial set of goals (career, marriage, family), may be called by an inner necessity to the painful and exacting process of individuation.

"The Rootwalker," the last poem of *Snapshots,* is a redefinition of psychological and poetic perspective. No longer does it seem "worth while to lay— / with infinite exertion— / a roof I can't live under," and the previous stratagems seem "blueprints, / closings of gaps, measurings, calculations"—all useless now that

> A life I didn't choose
> chose me: even
> my tools are the wrong ones
> for what I have to do.

4. In the original essay, "Prospective Immigrants Please Note" was quoted in full; in this volume it appears on p. 21.

Already she has begun to try out a language more expressive of
the uncertainties of a bold conception of selfhood;

> I'm naked, ignorant,
> a naked man fleeing
> across the roofs
> who could with a shade of difference
> be sitting in the lamplight
> against the cream wallpaper
> reading—not with indifference—
> about a naked man
> fleeing across the roofs.

The marvellous pun on "difference/indifference" effects the transi-
tion from the literate observer to the roofwalker, "exposed, larger
than life, / and due to break my neck." The phrase "larger than life"
suggests not just his heroism but the recognition that, ignorant as he
is, he is exposing himself to the dangers and mysteries not just of
personal destiny but of existence itself.

The "difference" in perspective calls into question society's as-
sumptions about men and women both separately and in relation to
each other. "A Marriage in the 'Sixties" refuses the clichés of con-
jugal devotion and brings love complicated by intelligence to a sepa-
rate yet shared existence. "Antinöus: The Diaries" and "Rustication"
express, even more viscerally than "Snapshots," a revulsion against
the middle-class, suburban life which traps women, either willingly
or helplessly, in gestures and postures. In "Antinöus" Rich speaks
through the mask of a man, but as the favorite of the Emperor Had-
rian, memorialzed in busts for his sensual beauty, Antinöus becomes
the perverted image of the object of man's lust, and so a mirror of
a decadent society.

> If what I spew on the tiles at last,
> helpless, disgraced, alone,
> is in part what I've swallowed from glasses, eyes,
> motions of hands, opening and closing mouths,
> isn't it also dead gobbets of myself,
> abortive, murdered, or never willed?

In reaction against the definitions of "woman" allowed by the
rules of the game Rich at first identifies the new possibilities of self-
realization with "masculine" qualities within herself and so with
images of men in several poems near the end of the book. In "Al-
ways the Same" Prometheus "bleeds to life" and his heroic song is
described in a phrase from Lawrence. In "Likeness" the good man
whom the song tells us is hard to find is "anarchic / as a mountain
freshet / and unprotected / by the protectors." The "larger than
life" roofwalker is a naked man. Their masculine strength derives

not from mere physical courage but from the power of mind and
will and judgment. "Ghost of a Chance" pits a man's discriminating
intellect against the backward suck of the female sea, undifferen-
tiated and undifferentiating.[5] The rhythms of the middle lines imi-
tate the strained effort to emerge into air, and the monosyllable of
the last word-line, climaxing the long drag of the previous line,
suggests the satisfaction which comes from the oblivion of the sea's
triumph—a satisfaction which makes resistance all the more urgent.
At the end of "Snapshots" the woman, cutting cleanly through the
currents, is linked with "mind" and "light": "A woman sworn to
lucidity," as Adrienne Rich would later describe herself.

In Jungian psychology the poet is at this point imagining herself
in terms of her "animus," the archetypally "masculine" component
in the woman's psyche which corresponds to the "anima" or arche-
typally "female" component in the man's psyche. Each person, man
or woman, is a combination of—or, more accurately, an interaction
between—male and female characteristics; the anima in the man
and the animus in the woman express the dynamism of that inter-
action, which, if creative, will open the passage to an accommoda-
tion of opposites in an identity. So for the man the anima is the key
to the whole area of feeling and intuition and passion; "she" repre-
sents his relationship with matter, with sexuality, with the dark and
formless unconscious. Correspondingly, for a woman the animus
represents her affinity with light as mind and spirit and her capacity
for intellection and ego-consciousness. In the process of individua-
tion, then, activation of and engagement with the animus or anima
is generally the first major, and potentially dangerous, phase; it marks
the transition into a fuller realization of one's psychological being
and stands as the mediating point—one way or the other—which
makes hard-won selfhood possible. Whether initial differences be-
tween men and women in psychological character and orientation
are inherent or acculturated is a matter for specialists to continue
to investigate. Meanwhile Jung's terms provide at least a descriptive,
if not prescriptive, frame of reference within which to sort out the
different psychological dynamics through which men and women,
even sophisticated and aware men and women, struggle towards
androgynous wholeness.

One manifestation of this dynamic which neither Jungians nor
critics have yet examined is the fact that, with a frequency too regu-
lar to be ignored, artists have identified themselves, especially in
their capacity as artists, with their anima or animus, as the case may
be. One would not want to insist on this connection rigidly, but the
tendency is strong enough to suggest a pattern. And the reason

5. In the original essay, "Ghost of a Chance" was quoted in full; in this volume it
appears on p. 20.

would seem to be that the artistic process, a function of the process of self-realization, is thereby a function of the anima or animus in the psyche: the man breaking open the categories of consciousness to the ebb and flow of the unconscious, submitting the light to the darkness; the woman drawing the inchoate into shape, submitting emotion to the discriminating light. Poetry as a function of the anima or of the animus helps to illuminate the difference, for example, between Walt Whitman and Emily Dickinson or, to cite two contemporary poets who have been closely associated with each other, the difference between Robert Duncan and Denise Levertov. The fact that the Muses are women and anima-figures is just a sign that up till now art has been a dominantly masculine domain.

The psycholgical and artistic point which the *Snapshots* volume dramatizes is Adrienne Rich's rejection of the terms on which society says we must expend our existence and her departure on an inner journey of exploration and discovery. As a woman-poet, she finds herself, perhaps unconsciously to a large extent, making the initial discoveries in the dimension and through the lead of her animus. So in "Face" she finds her reflection in the painting of a man whose "eye glows mockingly from the rainbow-colored flesh." Yet this mirror-image is himself "a fish, / drawn up dripping hugely / from the sea of paint." The metaphor, with the pun on "drawn," establishes the connection between the artistic process and the interaction of consciousness and the unconscious. The unconscious is the reservoir whose elements need to emerge into conscious comprehension and definition, and the artist must draw them up into the "glow" and "flash" of the light "out of the blackness / that is your true element."

Such an attempt at reorientation has inevitably made tremendous differences in the kind of poem Adrienne Rich has been writing. She was herself very aware of the fact that a radical shift had occurred in her conception of the technique and construction of poems. In a previously unpublished introduction to a poetry reading given in 1964, between *Snapshots* and *Necessities of Life,* she summed up the transition. It deserves quotation in full as one of the remarkable statements about contemporary poetry; it describes not just the direction she would increasingly explore but also the controlling impulse of most of the poetry now being written.[6]

In other words, Rich has developed, as a poet, from a single-minded identification with the animus as a controlling consciousness which could secure itself in forms and suppress the threats to that security, to a reliance on the animus as the power within herself through which psychic experience with all its unknown turbu-

6. In the original essay, "Poetry and Experience" was quoted in full; in this volume it appears on p. 91.

lences and depths can emerge into articulation as the images and rhythms of the poem. Anne Bradstreet, our first poet, referred to herself, half playfully, as the mother of her poems; Adrienne Rich gives herself the more comprehensive role of parent. At the same time the animus is only the mediating point within the psyche; no matter how active it is, Adrienne Rich writes as a woman. "The Knight" describes the negative and destructive aspects of identification with the animus: an encasing of the flesh and nerves and even the eye in armor as cold as it is glittering. By contrast, perhaps the most dramatic image in *Snapshots* is the figure of the woman at the climax of the title poem. A 1964 poem published in *Necessities of Life* returns to Emily Dickinson and addresses her almost as the type of the woman-poet:

> you, woman, masculine
> in single-mindedness,
> for whom the word was more
> than a symptom—
>
> a condition of being.
> Till the air buzzing with spoiled language
> sang in your ears
> of Perjury
>
> and in your half-cracked way you chose
> silence for entertainment,
> chose to have it out at last
> on your own premises.

The pun on "premises" makes Dickinson's retreat to the family household a consequence of her resolution to live and write on her own terms in the face of public incomprehension like the critic Higginson's, and the irony is that her determination only made her seem "half-cracked" to Higginson, complacent in his masculine assumptions about what women and poets are.

Necessities of Life (1966), *Leaflets* (1969) and *The Will to Change* (1971) are better books than *Snapshots;* they move steadily and with growing success towards making a poetry which is not just an activity consonant with life but an act essential to it. "The Trees" is a good example of the development.[7]

Rich has commented on the importance of Williams' example in her learning not to be "self-protective" like Frost and thereby to "take the emotional risk as well as the stylistic risk." But the emotional and psychological quality of her verse is utterly her own, and the prosody shows none of the posturing of much "experimental" verse and none of the halting choppiness which too deliberate a pre-

---

7. In the original essay, "The Trees" was quoted in full; in this volume it appears on pp. 25–26.

occupation with "breath-unit" imposes on some of Williams' follow-
ers. In "The Trees", the rhythms trace out the psychic movement,
doubling back on itself as it proceeds through a sequence of images.
The images, vivid and preternaturally clear, are not descriptive in
the usual sense. That is, they do not paint an actual scene or set up
a narrative situation; they compose an internal landscape, eerie but
strangely recognizable. Images of "eye" and "camera" persist
through *Necessities of Life,* but increasingly in the later volumes
dream and dream-imagery occur. And, as in a dream, the details
are so present that they convey the poet's involvement with the par-
ticulars of experience from which the dream-poem derives.

What, then, does the poem trace out? A movement from within
out, so that the empty forest "will be full of trees by morning." The
psyche is a house, a structure suggesting now a plantation and now
a hospital or sanatorium; but the house is filled with the natural and
primitive shapes of trees rooted in the earth beneath the floor-boards
and straining with a life of their own. While the conscious ego (the
"I" of the poem) conducts its accustomed correspondence, the trees
disentangle themselves and break out under the cover of darkness
into the open air, "like newly discharged patients / half-dazed, mov-
ing / to the clinic doors." Not that the external world appears
merely as the mirror of the individual psyche; the night and moon
and forest are out there from the beginning, and "the smell of
leaves and lichen" reaching "like a voice into the rooms" seems to
have initiated the trees' movement and the internal "whispers /
which tomorrow will be silent." The forest is empty to the individ-
ual until she realizes it, and the realization involves a distinctly per-
sonal and human awareness such as the forest cannot attain in and
of itself. The poem ends, as it began, in mystery, and the trees are
the exemplification of the mystery—the seemingly related mystery—
of the internal and external worlds. One becomes aware of the com-
plexities of one's becoming aware as well as of the complexities of
the things perceived. Now the moon that has shone whole in the
empty sky "is broken like a mirror, / its pieces flash now in the
crown / of the tallest oak." The poem has not unriddled the mind
or "reality" but rendered the encounter in a dreamscape for the
reader to encounter for himself.

At the same time the entire thrust of the poem is a clarification of
the uncomprehended or inadequately comprehended by recreating
what *exists* beyond paraphrase or abstraction; in the imagery of sev-
eral poems in *Necessities* light pierces darkness. Even here the moon,
shattered by the branches of the trees, still illuminates the night,
and the sun is the source of the rare moments of happiness and
release in the book: "In the Woods", "The Corpse-Plant", and
"Noon". In "Focus" Rich comes as close as she ever has to an ex-

plicitly religious dimension in the perception of things. Caught
in the "veridical light," falling on her desk-top through a skylight,

> an empty coffee-cup,
> a whetstone, a handkerchief, take on

> their sacramental clarity, fixed by the wand
> of light as the thinker thinks to fix them in the mind.

> O secret in the core of the whetstone, in the five
> pencils splayed out like fingers of a hand!

> The mind's passion is all for singling out.
> Obscurity has another tale to tell.

The intensity of Rich's poems since the late 'fifties stems precisely
from the mind's passion and from the fact that in her mind and pas-
sion test and confirm each other. The sacrament is the flash of the
mind as it fixes, camera-like, the everyday things caught in this un-
usual light.

For Rich, however, a deepening subjectivity does not mean with-
drawal, as it did for Dickinson, but, on the contrary, a more search-
ing engagement with people and with social forces. "Necessities of
Life", the first poem in that volume, notes her re-entry into the
world after a time of guarded isolation. A world still marred by
mutability ("Autumn Sequence", "Not Like That", "Side by Side",
"Moth Hour"), still scarred by the violences of human relationship
("The Parting", "Any Husband to Any Wife", "Face to Face") and
by the abuse of the environment ("Open Air Museum", "Breakfast
at a Bowling Alley in Utica, N.Y."), increasingly menaced by poli-
tics and war ("Spring Thunder"); in short, stained, as "The Knot"
tells us, by the blood-spot at the heart of things. *Necessities of Life*
is filled with elegies ("After Dark", "Mourning Picture", "Not Like
That"), and the title was meant, among other things "to suggest
the awareness of death under everything that we are trying to es-
cape from or that is coloring our responses to things, the knowledge
that after all time isn't ours." Existence is persistence, but these
poems are affirmations, in the extremity of our situation, of the will
to persist. "Like This Together", one of the best poems in the book,
concludes:

> Dead winter doesn't die,
> it wears away, a piece of carrion
> picked clean at last,
> rained away or burnt dry.
> Our desiring does this,
> make no mistake, I'm speaking
> of fact: through mere indifference
> we could prevent it.
> Only our fierce attention

> gets hyacinths out of those
> hard cerebral lumps,
> unwraps the wet buds down
> the whole length of a stem.

Again against "indifference," "our fierce attention": only through that can the world last into the next season; we survive or perish together.

As an expression of this conviction, Rich's politics have taken clearer shape. The rejection of bourgeois mores voiced in *Snapshots* has led to a more radical view of the necessity, for life, of re-ordering social values and structures. But even the political poems in *Leaflets* and *The Will to Change* (for example, "For a Russian Poet", "Implosions", the "Ghazals", "The Burning of Paper Instead of Children") are not, in the end, propaganda leaflets. They remain poems because Rich has too powerful a sense of "original sin" to make the utopian mistake of externalizing evil by projecting it on others. The poems compel us precisely because they record how excruciating it is to live in this time and place; the politics is not abstracted and depersonalized but tested on the nerve-ends. The psychological and political revolutions are interdependent, because personal and public tragedy are linked, as "The Burning of Paper Instead of Children" and "The Photograph of the Unmade Bed", as well as the title poem, declare. Individually and collectively we need "the will to change."

As the ultimate challenge to her initial assumptions, Adrienne Rich raises the dreaded question for a poet: the very validity and efficacy of language. Is art the act of clarification and communication that we say it is? As early as "Like This Together" in 1963 she was worrying that "our words misunderstand us." Now in "The Burning of Paper":

> What happens between us
> has happened for centuries
> we know it from literature
>
> still it happens
>
> . . . .
>
> there are books that describe all this
> and they are useless

If language has no power to affect the given, then is the resort to language an evasion of action, as the revolutionaries charge? The epigraph to the poem quotes Fr. Daniel Berrigan: "I was in danger of verbalizing my moral impulses out of existence." Only unsparing honesty permits an artist to contemplate such a dangerous question, but Rich confronts it again and again through the last two books. "Shooting Script" speaks of "the subversion of choice by language." "The Burning of Paper" imagines "a time of silence / or few words," when touch might be more immediate, and quotes Antonin Artaud: *"burn the texts."*

Yet this damning self-examination is conducted in the words of poems which are urgent, even desperate attempts at clarification and communication. Not that the questioning has been vain: there must be no blinking away the dangers of language as escape or the tenuousness of any attempt at articulation. But in the acknowledgment of all these limits, language remains a human *act* which makes other actions and choices possible: "Only where there is language is there world," "We are our words" ("The Demon Lover"); "Our words are jammed in an electric jungle; / sometimes, though, they rise and wheel croaking above the treetops" ("Ghazals"); "I am thinking how we can use what we have / to invent what we need" ("Leaflets"); "I wanted to choose words that even you / would have to be changed by" ("Implosions"). So, even in "The Burning of Paper", "this is the oppressor's language / yet I need it to talk to you." The conclusion is not to stop speaking and writing but to make words penetrate to the will as well as the mind and heart: "the fracture of order / the repair of speech / to overcome this suffering" ("The Burning of Paper").

In other words, persistence requires relocation. Much has intervened between *A Change of World* and *The Will to Change*. In "Storm Warnings" Rich had strategically enclosed herself within protective walls; now with the apocalypse perhaps about to break over our heads, she insists that we not merely submit but actively commit ourselves to change, as persons and as a people.

The poem as snapshot is no longer enough: stasis is death. "Pierrot Le Fou" begins:

> Suppose you stood facing
> a wall
>   of photographs
> from your unlived life
>
> as you stand looking at these
> stills from an unseen film?

It quickly becomes clear that the poem is concerned with, and is working as, film rather than photograph; "Pierrot le Fou" is itself a film by Jean-Luc Godard. Not that there is more narrative in these new poems; in fact, there is generally less, just as in most serious films there has been a reduction, almost an elimination, of plot for the imaging of a psychic dream-world. So in Rich's poetry there is a tendency toward longer poems or more sustained sequences of pieces; and they operate, even more exclusively than before, as a juxtaposition of images, spaced out on the page so that the sensibility can react and make connections. The poems of *The Will to Change* are a refinement of the imagistic technique worked out in the "Ghazals" of *Leaflets,* about which Rich has observed that "the continuity and unity flow from the associations and images playing back and forth. . . ." The title of the volume is from Charles Olson, and without being in any way an imitation of Olson these poems are Rich's exploration of "composition by field" so that the poem occupies the page on which it is placed as the ideogrammic expression of how her mind occupies the world in which and on which it operates. One of the purest instances of the technique is the first section of "Shooting Script".[8] The effect is not a static list of images but a flow of interacting and mutually clarifying images: at once linear and encircling, defining temporally an area of dreamscape or poemscape.

"The Photograph of the Unmade Bed" explicitly distinguishes the poem from the snapshot: the poem says, or should say, "This could be"; the photograph says "This was," and is therefore a "photograph of failure." "Images for Godard", the succeeding poem in the book, is important for sketching out her developing intentions. Section I renders the search for meaning through language in the familiar cinematic metaphor of driving through a contemporary city. Section 2 compiles a montage of camera-shots. Section 3 links love with the ability to change and move toward the other person; love is, or ought to be, a kind of movie, but it is constantly being "stopped," so that connections are only achieved at moments. So Section 4 admits the limitations of what the artist, Godard in particular, has been able to achieve thus far; he ends his film *Alphaville* with the words "I love you" but cannot proceed from there because by his own declarations he cannot make a movie about love, only about the striving toward love. But the final section projects the possibility of the movie-poem that Godard had failed at:

> the mind of the poet is the only poem
> the poet is at the movies
>
> dreaming the film-maker's dream but differently
> free in the dark as if asleep
>
> free in the dusty beam of the projector
> the mind of the poet is changing
>
> the moment of change is the only poem

But is the change only dream? Are dreams realities? "Shooting Script" is the scenario for the movie-poem. It consists of two parts of seven sections each. Part I intimates a "fresh beginning" but is

---

8. In the original essay, "Shooting Script," section 1, was quoted in full; in this volume it appears on pp. 54–55.

dominated by a sense of past failures whch trap the mind and im-mobilizc "simple choice." Section 8, the opening of Part II, sees what has gone before as "a poetry of false problems, the shotgun wedding of the mind, the subversion of choice by language" and from this point on there is greater and greater insistence on the fu-ture as the dimension of choice. The past is associated with photo-graphs (section 10) and even with film (section 9), or at least with a mere "Newsreel' of where one has been. In "Images for Godard", the movement of love had been "stopped, to shoot the same scene / over & over." "A Valediction Forbidding Mourning" referred to "the experience of repetition as death." Now the last section of "Shooting Script" rejects "whatever it was, the image that stopped you, the one on which you came to grief, projecting it over & over on empty walls," gives up "the temptations of the projector," and ends with the charge to move on: "To pull yourself up by your own roots; to eat the last meal in your old neighborhood." The shooting of the movie-poem has been so functional that it has had the effect of making the vital connection between art and life. As early as "The Diamond Cutters" Rich had warned the artist to concentrate on the work ahead rather than past achievements. But this is some-thing more: here the poem is necessary as the moment of change, and it validates itself by propelling the poet, and us, past the poem into that open space where some act besides words may map out the future.

In approaching the point of individual decision the words act as outward thrusts of communication. This is a poetry of dialogue and of the furious effort to break through to dialogue: "I want your secrets—I *will* have them out" ("The Demon Lover"); "We're fight-ing for a slash of recognition / a piercing to the pierced heart. / Tell me what you are going through—" ("Leaflets");

> I'd rather
> taste blood, yours or mine, flowing
> from a sudden slash, than cut all day
> with blunt scissors on dotted lines
> like the teacher told.
>
> ("On Edges")

The poems probe at the lesions between "I" and "you," and the "you" addressed is a particular person, or the reader, or an aspect of the poet—or all three at once. The aggressiveness of the imagery is a measure of the poet's frustrated animus; but the violence mea-sures as well the effort at contact and release, and the point of verbal contact, if achieved, is the moment of identification and change which is the aim and function and end of language.

The imagery associated wth self shifts in the last two books: a sign from the deeps. The animus is the cross-over point, leading in the direction of a fuller comprehension and integration of the self; so crucial is the stimulus it provides that, as we have seen, the individual at first tends to see herself in terms of the animus. After a time, however, she begins to see that the animus represents only an element, or range of capacities, to be assimilated into her identity as a woman. The poems of *Leaflets* and *The Will to Change* render just that transition in the conception of the self. "Orion", the first piece in *Leaflets,* is an animus poem. In reaction against the entanglements of domestic routine ("Indoors I bruise and blunder") Rich projects her sense of identity on the masculine presence of the constellation Orion, as she had since girlhood: first as her "genius" ("My cast-iron Viking, my helmed / lion-heart king in prison"); then as her "fierce half-brother," weighed down by his phallic sword; now as her mirror-image and apotheosis. Moreover, she is specifically identifying herself as poet with Orion; while writing the poem, she had in mind an essay by the German poet Gottfried Benn on the plight of the modern artist.

"The Demon Lover", written two years later, presents a more complex analysis. Here "he" is the "other": both the animus and the man who in refusing to recognize her animus compounds her own sense of division; the whole question is whether an accommodation with "him" is possible internally or externally:

> If I give in it won't
> be like the girl the bull rode,
> all Rubens flesh and happy moans.
> But to be wrestled like a boy
> with tongue, hips, knees, nerves, brain . . .
> with language?

Her animus is the sticking-point: for her to insist upon and for the man to negate. Her contention is not to be a man but a whole woman and as a woman to be taken fully into account. But the circumstances show "him" as adversary; not only does the "man within" appear as "demon lover," but the masculine lover becomes a demon because he clings to the simple opposition between mind and body which makes for the simple distinction between man and woman. In denying her mind and spirit, he must deny his passions and debase his body to lust. The quandary within and without remains unresolved; "he," animus and lover, refuses her his secrets and consigns her to the female element: "Sea-sick, I drop into the sea."

Although to the demon lover she has seized on the terms which make connection most difficult, she has defined the only terms on which relation is possible. Neither man nor woman can be free until each has acknowledged the other. Adrienne Rich's new poems show an absorption of animus-powers into a growing sense of identity as woman and identification with women, and consciousness is the key. "Women" describes three images of self as "my three sisters," and comments: "For the first time, in this light, I can see who they are." "Planetarium" evokes the astronomer Caroline Herschel, her fame eclipsed by her brother William, as a heroine in the history of women's coming to consciousness, the light of her "virile" eye meeting the stellar light; of herself, Rich concludes:

> I am an instrument in the shape
> of a woman trying to translate pulsations
> into images   for the relief of the body
> and the reconstruction of the mind.

In a hypnotic poem called "I Dream I'm the Death of Orpheus", she adapts imagery from Jean Cocteau's movie about Orpheus to depict herself as a woman whose animus is the archetypal poet.[9] The strong, incantatory rhythms—a significant new development in some of the recent poems—work their magic. What the dream-poem traces out is the resurrection of Orpheus through the woman's determination to resist all depersonalizing forces—psychological, political, sexual—arrayed against the exercise of her powers. The animus-poet comes alive again within the psyche, and his return is a sign of, and a measure of, her ability to "see through" and move forward on her "mission": not the course laid out by the "authorities" as the safe way to remain intact but the one intimated by "the fulness of her powers" as the only way to deliver herself whole. At this point in her life and in history such a purpose puts her against prevailing conditions and makes for lonely dislocation. Orpheus revives within her "on the wrong side of the mirror," "learning to walk backward against the wind."

But the contrary direction is not negative; bent on affirming life's possibilities, it makes the friction bearable and transfiguring. "We're living through a time / that needs to be lived through us," she writes in "The Will to Change", and that is the reverse of Matthew Arnold's perception of the modern paralysis as the feeling that everything is to be endured and nothing to be done.

The process is not, of course, completed, nor can it be: Selfhood is the motive and end of the journey. But the fact that hers is not merely a private struggle but a summons to us all—at least to all of us who enter the door and cross the threshold into the psyche in- forms the poetry with a mythic dimension in a singularly demythologized time. A myth not because her experience has been appended, by literary allusion, to gods and goddesses, but because her experience is rendered so deeply and truly that it reaches common impulses and springs, so that, without gods and goddesses, we can participate in the process of discovery and determination. It is existen-

9. In the original essay, "I Dream I'm the Death of Orpheus" is quoted in full; in this volume it appears on pp. 50–51.

tialism raised to a mythic power, and the myth has personal and political implications. The result is a restoration to poetry of an ancient and primitive power, lost in the crack-up which the last centuries have documented. The power of the bard in his tribe has long since declined with the power of prophecy. Adrienne Rich's mission is to live out her dream of a society of individual men and women. By challenging us to a more honest realization, she has recovered something of the function of the poet among his people: not by transmitting their legends and tales but by offering herself—without pretensions, with honest hesitations—as the mirror of their consciousness and the medium of their transformation. In effect, her poetry has come to represent a secular and unillusioned vision of the poet as prophet and the prophet as scapegoat living out individually the possibilities of the collective destiny. By long tradition in the patriarchal culture this tribal function has been the prerogative of male poets, but there is something peculiarly clarifying and liberating about confronting ourselves through the mind and imagination of a woman. Equally so for men as for women, because the work of a woman-artist is much more likely than the work of most men to present the counter-image essential to his wholeness and to activate and call into play that whole area of emotion and intuition within himself which is the special province of the "woman within."

All this accounts for the centrality of Adrienne Rich's work in the contemporary scene, for the electric immediacy of the reader's or hearer's response, and for the finally healing effect of poems wracked with the pain of awareness and the pain of articulation.

ROBERT BOYERS

On Adrienne Rich: Intelligence and Will †

The title of Adrienne Rich's sixth and most recent book of poems is *The Will To Change*. As a title it declares emphatically the centrality of that will in the poet's life and work, and indeed, it has provided an unmistakable thrust in the poems she has written since 1958 or so. Now it seems to me that most of our contemporaries value this will to change all too much, not because they are politically radical or personally nimble and adventurous in any striking way, but because such a will has taken on the qualities of an ideological fashion. To be sure, fashions in the realm of intellect do necessarily bespeak particular emotional commitments and frames of mind, and may not therefore be reduced to the status of intellec-

† From *Salmagundi*, 22–23 (Spring-Summer, 1973), 132–148. Reprinted by permission of the author.

tual phenomena pure and simple. But we know that ideological fashions frequently detach themselves from underlying emotional factors and assume in time a life and momentum of their own. So important is the will to change in Adrienne Rich's mature work that it may well serve as primary focus in any consideration of her poetry, for it is her understanding and treatment of the ideological dynamics involved that will have much to say about the kind of intelligence we respond to as we read the successive volumes. At the same time, we must try to do justice to the wide range of insights, indeed to the variety of wills, represented in this very singular poetry.

The poet has had an abiding sense of her life and work as split in a decidedly simple and predictable way. As a young woman she had thought of herself as neat and decorous, cultivating a solid look, "Neither with rancor at the past/ Nor to upbraid the coming time," as she described it wistfully in "At Majority" (1954). In those years, things had a certain weight and poems could express them in all their apparent accustomedness and density. It was not as though the young poet were entirely unaware of the abyss of uncertainty, but she had a confident way of holding it off, of handling it elegantly so that it seemed at most a mildly threatening idea. Her poetic skills, lavishly praised in the early '50's by Auden and Jarrell among others, seemed altogether a match for any difficult notions or untoward sensations that might have disturbed that wonderful poise and control, whether of self or of the aesthetic medium. All at once, though, in the poems of the late '50's, a more embattled and urgent air began to creep in, and the poet discovered that she had been covering up, not controlling merely, but wilfully evading. There is a certain tidiness in the discovery as she seeks to evoke it in the volume *Snapshots of a Daughter-in-Law* (1963), but we know in the perspective of subsequent volumes that the experience was in fact deeply important to the poet. Where in 1954 she could announce: "Now knowledge finds me out;/ in all its risible untidiness/ it traces me to each address,/ dragging in things I never thought about" ("From Mourning Glory To Petersburg"), she handles her material much more substantively, if still a bit programmatically, in "The Roofwalker" (1961).[1]

The single controlling image demanding control of all particulars in a given poem is perhaps the most consistent element in the volume *Snapshots,* and accounts for the still formal quality we sense in the various poems. They deliver up their treasures rather too explicitly, we feel, and the note of discovery becomes so pointed and anticipated that we are grateful even for outbursts of spite or anger that break the pattern. But best of all are the rare introductions of specific tensions the poet wishes to work through rather than to re-

1. In the original essay, "The Roofwalker" was quoted in full; in this volume it appears on pp. 19–20.

solve. In the ten-part title poem (1958–1960) she asks of herself, of women generally, "Pinned down/ by love, for you the only natural action,/ are you edged more keen/ to prise the secrets of the vault? has Nature shown/ her household books to you, daughter-in-law,/ that her sons never saw?" There is no clamoring here for definitive answers, no triumphant declarations of the courage to change as though change were all one could conceivably ask of anyone truly human. The poet's self-concern here is seemly and reasonable. She wants to know about herself, her secrets, her gifts. She does not speak yet as though perpetual motion were the ideal state, the will to change the index of perfect maturity. Her business, to the degree that she can make it out, is to feel herself, to think beyond formal categories, to reject whatever is merely habitual on behalf of what she can discover as potentially to be won. Most important of all, she does not blithely reject the past as though it had nothing to tell, nor dismiss orderliness and the clean lines of a modest behavior for undifferentiated passion. The lust to be wholly contemporary has not yet become dangerously compelling.

In what is surely her best book to date, *Necessities of Life* (1966), Adrienne Rich moves steadily to inhabit the world and to make contact with that self she had thought largely repressed and almost forgotten. It is a volume not so much of youthful discovery as of sobering expansiveness, a coming out into a challenging universe armed with all the gifts of steady vision and confident warmth we associate only with a very mature person. Adrienne Rich achieves in the poems of this volume a dignity and casual elevation that are altogether rare in the poetry of any period. Imagination here is in the service of intelligence in a way that might well dampen the poetic ardor of most poets, more committed as they are to the sheer vagrancies of creative inspiration. The remarkable thing about the poems in *Necessities,* though, is that they betray no decline of invention, no thinning of poetic texture, nothing in the way of mere reasonable constraint. They are rich in a quality I can only call character. They bear, everywhere, the marks of a rare and distinguished personhood which we take as at least an implicit celebration of our being. But the poems themselves can say ever so much better what I mean to describe. Here is "After Dark" (1964), of which it would be unfair to quote less than the full text.[2]

The echoes in such a poem serve only to enhance one's sense of its largeness, its breadth of vision and informed intelligence. Nothing in the way of irrelevant local texture removes our concern from the very grave and beautiful relation that is evoked, a relation that is as much a communing of a soul with itself as it is the working out of

2. In the original essay, "After Dark" was quoted in full; in this volume it appears on pp. 28–30

affections between the generations. The tension here is not between idea and image, between abstraction and concretion, but between what we know and what we feel. It is the business of the poem to do justice to both, to see to it that the one is at least to some degree informed by the other. There is no pristine self here, no absolutely authentic being the discovery of which is exclusively potentiated by a cutting loose from all that is customary and embedded. How gratifying that the father's actual or imagined *"I know you better/ than you know yourself"* should be dealt with not by way of severe rejection or denial, but in the context of the words, "woke up one morning/ and knew myself your daughter./ Blood is a sacred poison." Relation is something we make, to be sure, but it may be conferred as well, and this the poet gracefully acknowledges in the poem as a way of coming to terms with her own inclinations. As she ponders the relationship, projects for herelf a consoling vision of it that is at once conclusive and fragrantly evocative, her associations become progressively literary, but there is no ounce in them of the inauthentic. The poetic echoes refresh the context by reminding us of comparably moving treatments of similar themes. At one point she exclaims, "no more to scourge my inconsistencies—" and we think of Lowell's farewell to his grandfather in *Life Studies*. Or, as we read the first three stanzes of part two, we think of Sylvia Plath's ritualistic efforts to make contact with her father. Or we call to mind Lear's farewell to Cordelia as we ponder such lines as "I'll sit with you there and tease you/ for wisdom, if you like," and so on. This is a poetry that can afford such echoes, for as it is generous with its emotions without railing or ranting, so can it securely draw upon an entire tradition to substantiate its sincerity. In a work less open, less generous, the associations might seem insufficiently modulated or assimilated, perhaps even calculated. Here they strike us fine.

I have chosen to look at "After Dark" because it is a wonderful poem and because it illuminates by contrast what has lately happened in Adrienne Rich's work. We notice in this poem that the speaker is not pleased that "the sashcords of the world fly loose." Though she struggles to win her own sense of self, she yet feels the need to be known, to be seen if not quite seen through. How beautifully she puts her impulse in the line "I grow protective toward the world," for we understand that the impulse of which she speaks is nothing less than the mature desire to resume coherence in the face of progressive assaults on those stable props that constitute our necessity and at least part of our definition. That "blunt barge" is more than the vehicle of death here. It is, in fact, an emblem of that coming home to which each of us must incline, not in the sense that we simply resign ourselves to things as they are or to our eventual demise, but in the sense that we acknowledge what belongs, in-

escapably, to each of us. As the poet recalls the murderous fantasies
of childhood she senses—as she sensed when still a child—the de-
gree of her participation in her father's death, and we are impressed
with the profound ambivalence of most such relationships. The
poem's conclusion in no sense banishes this ambivalence, or resolves
it, but it allows for a final expression of affection that further vali-
dates the sincerity of that ambivalence.

* * *

If we ask what are the sources of such ambivalence, * * * we
should have to speak again of character, but also and more precisely
of the poet's sense of the rhythms of experience, the necessary al-
ternations of dream and reality in the life of the spirit, the cultivated
tension between knowing and feeling. In the poem "Not Like That"
(1965) the speaker woos a picturesque extinction, a deliberate for-
getfulness that prepares one for nullity of a most encompassing sort.
She envisions herself in a domesticated cemetery—"The turf is a
bedroom carpet"—and muses: "To come and sit here forever,/ a
cup of tea on one's lap/ and one's eyes closed lightly, lightly/ per-
fectly still/ in a nineteenth century sleep!/ it seems so normal to
die." As she works the shadows of the portrait, probing its secrets,
she concludes that it is not extinction she wants, but some soothing
vision of ultimacy such as we find perpetually available to us as
children. Perhaps it is the very availability of childish consolation
that announces to the older poet the insufficiency of those earlier
visions. This has nothing to do with simply growing up and accept-
ing the fact that we can no longer delude ourselves with childish
fancies. What the mature poet determines to banish is the tendency
to drift. She refuses to allow imagination to go its own way, to seek
its objects in any guise. Not just the fantasies, the easy consolations,
but the very time of childhood "was a dream too, even the oatmeal/
under its silver lid, dream-cereal/ spooned out in forests of spruce."
In the remarkable image of dream-cereal the poet tells us she refuses
to be nourished by anything patently insubstantial, rejects easy re-
gressions as the means to any satisfying identity. Such symbolic re-
turns have about them a death-like air when too regularly or lavishly
indulged, and the static portraiture of the seated figure, "eyes closed
lightly, lightly," surely stands in this regard as starkly emblematic
warning. Things are not still, not permanent, not easy, though we
are sometimes tempted by "the warm trickle of dream/ staining the
thick quiet"—a dazzling image bespeaking at once the coziness and
puerility of the all too available. The final lines are bracing: "The
drawers of this trunk are empty./ They are all out of sleep up here."

The rejection of the dream-life, the emergence into clarified per-
ception and knowing interaction with the things of this world, is

central to the poems of *Necessities*. The will to change is considered within a relatively stable context, for the poet here presupposes a way of life. It is nothing so exalted and distinctive as the old high way Yeats wistfully remembers in the poems of Coole Park or in the "Prayer" for his daughter, but it has its decided features. Chiefly these features have to do with a decision to work through one's problems, to be attentive to one's needs and to the shifting demands of one's environment and companions, to work always at breeding flowers from the refuse heap of the contemporary situation. Involved as well is a growing commitment to what might be called social reality, as though one could not legitimately expect to know oneself or to deal with one's personal limitations without considering the degree to which they are conditioned by external actualities. What we have quite frequently in these poems, and to a much greater extent in the later work, is the spectacle of a vivid intelligence working to avoid being overwhelmed by brute matter. In "Open-Air Museum" (1964) the poet wonders at frail flowers sprouting in the town dump, and feels she has been brought "face to face with the flag of our true country:/ violet-yellow, black-violet,/ its heart sucked by slow fire." Fragments of shattered dreams lie about, "the rose-rust carcass of a slaughtered Chevrolet," scraps of a photo-album, a three-wheeled baby carriage. But it is not the poet's function simply to mourn what is past, or to shake her fist at a civilization that betrays its best hopes. The emphasis of her poem lies in the lines "those trucked-off bad dreams/ outside the city limits/ crawl back in search of you." Her heart counsels that she listen carefully for the intermittent "Cry of truth among so many lies." There is no stratification of meaning here, no loose weaving together of various levels of intention that yet remain distinct, but a total human situation truly observed. The poem creates an enduring illusion of virtual experience, in Susanne Langer's terms. Our sense of the poem is of having entered a world that is whole and clearly related to the world we customarily inhabit, though not literally co-extensive with it. What we recognize, are never permitted to forget in Adrienne Rich's poems, is that the materials we are shown constitute events in the poet's mental and emotional life. We do not expect, and never feel that we get, transcriptions of reality such as a theory of verisimilitude might enjoin upon the artist. Nor do we get, or expect, discursive argument of a philosophical nature. All we are shown carries with it that peculiar baggage of associations and tensions that the poet customarily lugs around, as though it were strapped forever to her back. She may shift the weight from time to time, may dance about to lighten the load, may even, temporarily, forget her burden, but it is there, and she will acknowledge it in time.

In "Like This Together" (1963), the poet's understanding of her work as in some basic way a clarification of life, her own and others', is verified in a whole range of particulars. She informs us in a recent interview (*The Ohio Review*, 1972) that "what it means to be a man, what it means to be a woman . . . is perhaps the major subject of poetry from here on." But such an approach seems almost parochial set against the more embracing drive of "Like This Together" and comparable pieces. Not "what it means to be a woman" but how to preserve one's essential humanity is the underlying thrust of her poem. What threatens is the disintegration of the immediate physical landscape, an erosion of stable landmarks that leaves us without concrete roots, "sitting like drugged ducks/ in a glass case," unable to break out for want of identifiable objects towards which we may press ourselves to struggle. So the civic disaster, the blight of perpetual and empty urban renewals is a reminder of the hollowness of most other renewals undertaken in the spirit of escape. "They're tearing down the houses/ we met and lived in," she cries. ". . . soon our two bodies will be all/ left standing from that era." And on. It is a miserable scene, dank and impoverished, and it leaves the lonely soul with no recourse but to "old detailed griefs/ [that] twitch at my dreams," an aftermath of "miscarried knowledge." But it is not victimization that Adrienne Rich courts, despite her obvious affinities with the victims of recent confessional verse. She takes what we may call a more active approach to the body of her fate most of the time. The marvelous final stanza, part five of her poem, puts the case as follows.[3]

To read such a stanza is to have rather a sharp sense of how the world appears to a woman of intelligence and purpose, who is yet capable of considerable pain. It is a sequence of lines that impresses much more than affirmation, more than the blithe overcoming to which so many of our poets since Emerson have directed their energies. And, as an important aspect of its message is the exalting of "fierce attention," just so does the poem ask us for careful scrutiny if we would glean its fullness. In particular we shall need to address cautiously the lines: "Our desiring does this,/ make no mistake, I'm speaking/ of fact: through mere indifference/ we could prevent it." Prevent what? we may at first wonder. Prevent "dead winter"? "Our desiring"? Actually, of course, the poet refers to something we may call the impaling past, the past imperfectly apprehended that locks us into sterile patterns, rehearsed postures, that blocks our way when we would step out and experience ourselves as creatures of quite remarkable extension. Shall we be anything but creatures of "fierce attention," the poet wants to know, and she is well advised to ask, for indifference, a function of cultural disorder and the breakdown of established authority, is surely among the central blights of our period.

The 1969 volume *Leaflets* seems to me to mark a decline in the poet's career. There are some brilliant things in the volume, patches of exquisite writing, several perfectly achieved poems, but the sense one takes from the volume is of things coming apart, not the texture of the universe merely, but the fibre of the poet's attention. She seems, if I may say so, less careful about what she says. She says, in fact, silly things, of a sort we cannot easily ignore or attribute to passing inattention, while moving on to the nearest reassuring sentiment. When a mature and accomplished poet writes ("In The Evening," 1966): "The old masters, the old sources, haven't a clue what we're about,/ shivering here in the half-dark 'sixties," we are forced to stop and vent serious doubts about the entire enterprise. What is the poet after? She seems too shrewd for us to say it is simply rage or utter desperation that prompts her to declare the perfect uniqueness of her own burdened moment. Is human experience in general so radically disparate that even the old masters could fail to intimate our problems, provide us with a clue? Apparently the poet believes in the specialness of her experience, though frankly nothing she tells us seems to me in the least astonishing. But that is not really so important. What matters is why she feels compelled to make us feel we have no clues. She apparently does not wish to play the role of victim to the hilt, so that vulnerability is but one of the notes she regularly sounds. And even when indulging such a posture, she resists the temptation to wring it for all it's worth, so that she appears at once vulnerable and wryly ironic. In "Flesh And Blood" (1965) she begins with "A cracked walk in the garden,/ white violets choking in the ivy," and we anticipate a slightly off-beat but gruesome cataloguing of small disasters. We get instead some mild reminiscence and a line like "Nobody's seen the trouble I've seen/ but you." The play on the song title is casual and flat and encourages a kind of pleasurable if silently knowing, collaborative wink between poet and reader. The tone is similarly right and more or less satisfying in "Holding Out" (1965) with its flavor of Frost or David Wagoner, the word "maybe" hovering over every insight: "Maybe the stovepipe is sound,/ maybe the smoke will do us in/ at first—no matter." Why, then, the insistence upon the radical unfamiliarity of our vulnerability in poems like "In The Evening," a poem by the way, that bears more than slight resemblance to "Dover Beach," both in the dire situation it posits and in the persistent clinging together of the two central figures.

In *Leaflets* and in *The Will To Change*, Adrienne Rich labors, it would seem, under the notion that we are inevitably period-creatures, that to deny the fact is to deny our very being. She tells us in "The Demon Lover" (1966) that "A new/ era is coming in./ Gauche as we are, it seems/ we have to play our part." Taken by themselves, such lines surely point in but one direction. The fact is, though, that they may not be taken in isolation from a great many other lines which not only qualify but openly contradict them. What I conclude is that Adrienne Rich wishes with all her strength to be other than a period-creature. She wishes, that is, to retain that sense of self displayed so handsomely in *Necessities of Life*. The problem is that progressively she falls prey to ideological fashions like the will to change, so that, though she is too intelligent ever to mouth petty slogans, she allows herself to be violated by them. They touch her verse with an almost programmatic wand. The underlying energy and tension remain, but they grow less and less visible as the set assertions come staggering forward:

The friend I can trust is the one who will let me have my death.
The rest are actors who want me to stay and further the plot.

. . . .

If the mind of the teacher is not in love with the mind of the student,
he is simply practising rape, and deserves at best our pity.

. . . .

Leroi! Eldridge! Listen to us, we are ghosts
condemned to haunt the cities where you want
to be at home.

. . . .

I have learned to smell a *conservateur* a mile away:
they carry illustrated catalogues of all that there is to lose.

(quotations from "Ghazals," 1968)

To think that the poet who could write so persuasively of her father's loss, or her own hard-earned, satisfying growth, should be so snide about having something to lose. What can she be thinking when she writes of smelling "a *conservateur*"? Does the poet imagine that men who have something to lose are necessarily blind reactionaries? Does she hold at no value the fruits of a man's labors when he is able to taste and savor those fruits? I ask such questions not to suggest that the poet has lost her senses—far from that—but to suggest how charged she has become with the nauseous propaganda of the advance-guard cultural radicals. Such sentiments as I've quoted from Adrienne Rich's poems are not, I insist, serious expressions of her intelligence but reflections of a will to be contemporary, to please those who are nothing but contemporary and who therefore can have little sense of the proper gravity of the poetic art. Sincere they may well be, some of them, but the density of language, the gravity of the word well chosen and scrupulously employed are surely considerations beyond their characteristic sense of things. That Adrienne Rich should have "fallen in" with such models is greatly to be lamented, for her development as a poet cannot be a happy one under such an influence.

I say this recognizing full well that one is not supposed to confuse the content of poems with their specific value as poems. The idea does seem to me a little ridiculous, taken generally, but I can see the point of such an objection where the works of certain other poets are at issue. If a poet is a radical innovator who brings experimental resources to his craft that may alter the direction of poetry in his time, he is surely entitled to be examined in a special way. Or if the poet is possessed of a voice so grandly authoritative that it strikes us as in some sense the expression of an entire age, so again will we need to deal with it in a special way. Adrienne Rich is neither a radical innovator nor the voice of an age. We think of intelligence when we read her best work, and we miss that intelligence when we examine much of her recent verse. It is no use pretending that what she says does not matter, or oughtn't to, or is marginal, by comparison with the brightness and energy of her line or the sharpness of her diction. It matters to us as readers that she should speak of practising rape when "the mind of the teacher is not in love with the mind of the student." How many students have minds, we should wonder when confronted with such a line, that any sensitive and intelligent person could love? How many of us can love what we at best but barely know? When I repeat such questions to myself, particularly in connection with the work of someone I admire as much as Adrienne Rich, I try to recall other lines, better urgings from the same body of verse. I remember, for example, "How did we get caught up fighting the forest fire,/ we, who were only looking for a still place in the woods?" The quality of such a line is more than plaintive. It is touched, perhaps, by a certain pride, but it is not altogether misplaced, at least. The suggestion is that we could not but take our place fighting the blaze, and this is no doubt what many serious people feel. Such sentiments, as the heart of a poet's work, are surely acceptable provided that they are meaningfully hedged, provided that they are accompanied by other sentiments that sufficiently undercut or challenge them, so that readers are called upon for participation rather than unambiguous assent. Only in scattered poems do we feel the presence of this fruitful tension as we go through the last two volumes. One slight poem in *Leaflets* called "The Observer" (1968) quietly establishes the tension of which we speak, a tension that abides as much in the poet as in the poem. What impresses me about this poem as well is the measured coherence of the vision, a coherence no doubt impossible for the poet trying to capture the unstable rhythms of the contemporary western

scene. Where most often in *Leaflets* we have fragmentary observa-
tions, notations jotted in the tumult of manning the front-lines, here
we have a sense of something approaching duration, the picture to
be pondered in place of the frantic words trailing beyond our
grasp.[4] Other poems in *Leaflets* one ought to read, for pleasure and
provocation, include "5:30 A.M.," "The Key," "Abnegation," and
"Night-break."

We began by speaking of the centrality of the will to change in
Adrienne Rich's mature verse, and surely it is time we turned to that
subject as a central focus in what remains to be said here. It is
difficult to avoid such a turning in looking at the volume *The Will
To Change,* of course, but few are the readers who seem ready to
front the subject directly. A reviewer for *The New York Times Book
Review* spoke of the volume's ". . . tough distrust of completion,"
and declared that "The poems are about departures, about the pain
of breaking away from lovers and from an old sense of self." The
observations seem accurate enough, but they do not tell us much.
The poems in this recent volume are about more than departures.
They are about the will to be both self and other, to embody at once
both presence and possibility. They are, in fact, about the will not to
be left behind, not to be deluded, not to rest with one's achieve-
ments or comforts. "A man isn't what he seems but what he de-
sires:/ gaities of anarchy drumming at the base of the skull," she
tells us in one of "The Blue Ghazals" (1968). A familiar enough
idea, looked at casually, but why the insistence upon anarchy, we
should like to know. Why such further lines as "Disorder is natural,
these leaves absently blowing." Absence, disorder as natural: and
only a few years earlier she had spoken so fiercely of the blight
that is rampant disorder, of the indifference and inattention that per-
mit the wasting of our endowments. In another of "The Blue
Ghazals" the poet writes: "Everything is yielding toward a foregone
conclusion,/ only we are rash enough to go on changing our lives./
An Ashanti woman tilts the flattened basin on her head/ to let the
water slide downward: I am that woman and that/ water." The ter-
rible downward glide is evoked in these poems as an inevitability to
which we lend ourselves as a mark of honor, of lucidity. But to de-
scribe our drift as in some sense honorable is not to see how terrible
it is, I'm afraid, and I doubt the poet has lately stepped out of the
current long enough to attend to this problem. In "I Dream I'm the
Death of Orpheus" (1968) she presents "A woman feeling the full-
ness of her powers/ at the precise moment when she must not use
them/ a woman sworn to lucidity." What is this terrible lucidity, we
wonder, that it should prevent us from using our powers: some such

4. In the original essay, "The Observer" was quoted in full; this volume it appears
on p. 43.

thing occurs to us to ask as we move through any number of poems here.

As earlier intimated, the will to change is at the heart of Adrienne Rich's thought and work, and it has much to do with this terrible lucidity. For what the poet insists upon is nothing less than full revelation of every motive, every shabby instinct and cheap thrill that drives her on. Now it is customary today to applaud a whole host of writers, prophets and other culture-heroes for their frankness, and surely we do not need to be reminded of the degree to which frankness has become a salable commodity. There is nothing offensive or commercial in Adrienne Rich's poetry, but it shares with other contemporary work a quality of impatience and of rashness that is a little disappointing. She is too ready in her poems to see the "Meanings burnt-off like paint/ under the blow-torch" ("Our Whole Life," 1969). Oh, she knows the toll the blow-torch will take, writhes a good deal under its too steady heat and glare. What disturbs us is that she should have so little faith in the usefulness of resistance. For the *conservateurs* she had ready contempt, but for the anxious wielders of the blow-torch, for the more openly murderous of her own intellectual instincts, she has no strength to resist. She laments that we are "Always falling and ending/ because this world gives no room/ to be what we dreamt of being," but she mistrusts the very idea of being anything solid and loyal. How often does she tell us that change and the will to change are all. More and more I think of Adrienne Rich's recent project as a kind of perpetual hungering relieved by nothing at all, for nothing we take in can satisfy this hunger to know, to devour, to transform, to move on. In "Images for Godard" (1970) we read: "the notes for the poem are the only poem/ the mind collecting, devouring/ all these destructibles," and later, "free in the dusty beam of the projector/ the mind of the poet is changing/ the moment of change is the only poem." And is the only reality worth knowing about, apparently.

The effect of all this on Adrienne Rich's writing has not been good, for though the poet need not manifest the organic wholeness of the traditional novelistic vision, obviously, she is responsible for more than a series of intensely noted fragments. There is some pleasure in watching her manage her combination of intimate detail and abstract rumination, in pondering her attempt to forge an authentic language deserving of the name dialogue, but we are impressed by the absence of that steady largeness of vision, those marked traits of character formed and expanding, that we marveled at in her earlier writing. The will to change has turned the poet from wholeness to analytic lucidity. Or perhaps it would be more appropriate to say that, unable to live according to these calmly alternating rhythms we think of as the emblem of a poised maturity, the poet has had to turn to the will to change to validate her hungers, to provide the stamp of authenticity she sought. I don't know for certain. What seems to me clear is that a point has been passed beyond which the poet has ceased to be herself, that blend of instinct and learned wisdom, innocent eye and educated adult, who knew there was a limit to will, and worth in steadfastness. Now that she has begun to speak of nature, of doing her thing, giving herself to the performance of "something very common, in my own way," I don't know that we may hope for very much from her verse beyond striking fragments. I shall have to hope for a resumption of that other toughness so well expressed in "Snapshots of a Daughter-in-Law." It may be fitting to conclude with a few lines from that poem, to remind ourselves of the course we have traveled:

> mere talent was enough for us—
> glitter in fragments and rough drafts
>
> . . . .
>
> our mediocrities over-praised,
> indolence read as abnegation,
> slattern thought styled intuition,
> every lapse forgiven . . .

Those of us who believe in the altogether special and distinguished qualities of Adrienne Rich's best work will not, I hope, forgive lightly her recent lapses, nor praise overmuch her more indulgent intuitions.

HELEN VENDLER

Ghostlier Demarcations, Keener Sounds †

Adrienne Rich's memorable poetry has been given us now, a book at a time, for twenty-two years. Four years after she published her first book, I read it in almost disbelieving wonder; someone my age was writing down my life. I felt then, as I feel now, that for each reader there are only a few poets of whom that is true, and by the law of averages, those poets are usually dead or at least far removed in time and space. But here was a poet who seemed, by a miracle, a twin: I had not known till then how much I had wanted a contemporary and a woman as a speaking voice of life:

> Strength came where weakness was not known to be,
> At least not felt; and restoration came

† From *Parnassus: Poetry in Review*, II, 1 (Fall–Winter, 1973), 5–10, 15–16, 18– 24. Reprinted by permission of the publisher.

> Like an intruder knocking at the door
> Of unacknowledged weariness.

When I look back now through *A Change of World* (1951), I try to remember which of the pages so held me and why; and I find four sets of poems I greet with the sense of *déja vu*. One set had simply lovely lines, seeming today almost too decorative, too designed, but presenting to me then the poetry of the delicately apprehended and the exquisitely remembered, poetry of "the flecked leaf-gilded boughs," and "paths fern-fringed and delicate," ornamented with "whisking emerald lizards." I did not mind, in some of these solacing poems, echoes of Auden or Yeats, feeling that what was beautiful was beautiful no matter who invented it; but there was, it was true, an ominous note which kept being interlaced with the poised rhythms.

A second group of poems set the status quo against some threatened future time; yet the danger was contained, and in fact the action of containing danger was gravely obligatory, a sacred trust. The poems articulated their own balance between danger and decorum in imagery of rebellion (which usually lost) against tradition (which usually won, at least tonally). The speaker for tradition in one poem is "the uncle in the drawing room"; gesturing towards "crystal vase and chandelier," knowing the "frailties of glass," he points seriously to the duties of the custodians of culture.[1] The poet-observer creating the uncle may see him ironically in part, but there is no denying the ethical imperative of his last claim. Equally subversive of tradition but yearningly attached to its honor, "For the Felling of a Tree in Harvard Yard" ends ambiguously on a double set of responses:

> The second oldest elm is down.

> The shade where James and Whitehead strolled
> Becomes a litter on the green.
> The young men pause along the paths
> To see the axes glinting bold.

> Watching the hewn trunk dragged away,
> Some turn the symbol to their own,
> And some admire the clean dispatch
> With which the aged elm came down.

Though revolution may end this poem, nostalgia rules it, nostalgia for the "roots enormous in their age," for "the great spire . . . overthrown." In 1955 I read this poem purely as elegy (no doubt confusing it in my undiscriminating admiration with "Binsey Poplars" and the spreading chestnut tree) and I was unable as yet, myself, to conceive of revolutionary impatience. But even now its tone

---

1. In the original essay, "The Uncle Speaks in the Drawing Room" was quoted in full; in this volume it appears on pp. 2–3.

seems to contain far more of the pang of elegy than of the briskness of destruction. So the poems played with fire, yet did not burn: I must have liked that.

The third set of poems that moved me then were poems on the identity and lot of women. I had no conscious thoughts on the topic, the natural order of the universe seeming then to be the inequality of man and woman; and yet some strains of discord in the book must have seemed an external documentary to those inarticulate strains in myself. On the one hand, woman was to be Patience on a monument, a Hermione-statue always there when her husband chose to come back.[2] Hard it may be, but learn it she must, says this poem; and it assumes that there is no such "estranged intensity" where *she* could be mentally foraging alone, and whence he might forbear to call *her* back. And yet, in other poems, the imperative of exploration, separation, private discovery, is equally felt:

> Each his own Magellan
> In tropics of sensation. . . .
> These are latitudes revealed
> Separate to each.
> ("Unsounded")

In still other poems, needlework, that laborious confection of female artistry, becomes the repeated symbol of the ambiguously triumphant womanly lot. While their lords left for "harsher hunting on the opposite coast," Norman ladies

> sat at home
> To the pleasing minor airs of lute and hautbois,
> While the bright sun on the expensive threads
> Glowed in the long windless afternoons.

But what is left of the Anglo-Norman battles but the Bayeux tapestry, which "prove[d]/ More than the personal episode, more than all/ The little lives" ("Mathilde in Normandy"). And, in spite of the seductive evenings in "The Kursaal at Interlaken," the female speaker, while playing her social rôle, nonetheless casts longing eyes toward a solitary virginity:

> Jungfrau, the legendary virgin spire,
> Consumes the mind with mingled snow and fire

* * *

But most of *A Change of World* is written by a girl in love, a girl "receiving marvels, signs":

> There is a streetcar runs from here to Mars.
> I shall be seeing you, my darling, there,

2. In the original essay, "An Unsaid Word" was quoted in full; in this volume it appears on p. 3.

Or at the burning bush in Harvard Square.
                        ("Vertigo")

This seems too easy an apotheosis now, but it seemed bold at first
reading, and drew me by the same authority as the lines in "For
the Conjunction of Two Planets" which imperiously declared for
myth against astrophysics:

> Whatever register or law
> Is drawn in digits for these two,
> Venus and Jupiter keep their awe,
> Warders of brilliance, as they do
> Their dual circuit of the west—
> The brightest planet and her guest.

Not only was our feminism only an occasional shadow over our
expectation of the ecstatic, our sense of permanent location in our
lot was only incipient, too. The fourth set of poems that kept me
standing in the library stacks reading this new and revelatory book
was the set about Europe. In *A Change of World* Rich struck all
the notes of her generation's inchoate responses to Europe: an at-
tachment, a disloyalty; beauty, decadence; the perfect, the tired;
art, the artificial. Alienated by a lengthily educated childhood from
the American scene, and yet invisibly, visibly, and irrevocably
American, the students who went abroad like Rich wandered tranced
in the deceptive paradises of the transatlantic escape.

Now, six books later, almost two decades older, Rich's readers
encounter her newest book, *Diving into the Wreck*. If we suspend
knowledge of what came between, we may ask what has happened
to the girl of 1951, that girl who wanted everything suffused by
the delicate and the decorative, who questioned her passivity even
while exhorting herself to that virtue, who mourned change and
yet sensed its coming, who feared her own alienation in her native
country, who, above these cares and anxieties, took pains that all
her poems should turn out right, that there should be no ragged
edges, that chimes should chasten discords—what has become of
her? She has forgotten, or repudiated, her dream of Europe.
Beethoven makes a fugitive appearance in the new book, but even
he is not permitted to represent nineteenth-century European high
culture; Rich calls her Beethoven poem "The Ninth Symphony of
Beethoven Understood at Last as a Sexual Message." Passivity, too,
is repudiated in principle, but returns in surreptitious forms, as
life is consumed by that which nourished it:

> Time takes hold of us like a draft
> upward, drawing at the heats
> in the belly, in the brain

> ... the mirror of the fire
> of my mind, burning as if it could go on
> burning itself, burning down
>
> feeding on everything
> till there is nothing in life
> that has not fed that fire
> ("Burning Oneself Out")

The overtones here come from Williams' "Burning the Christmas Greens," but Williams' poem is about the desire for change which consigns the greens to the fire, while Rich is helplessly suspended in the fires of time and thought. The old decorativeness reappears in the intricate ending, but this time not in the service of a scrim-curtain prettiness. As for the questions of female identity and the rival claims of change and tradition, they have merged into one inextricable and apparently insoluble problem. In the first book, change could be chosen or not; by now, Rich utters ruin (and resurrection) as inevitable law.

* * *

There is more to look at in *Diving into the Wreck,* notably its last poem; but first, in order to see the place of this book in Adrienne Rich's continuing writing, writing unflaggingly done through youth, marriage, motherhood, solitude, employment, political engagement, and fame, we must look back to earlier works. Except for youth, any one of these phases, not to speak of all of them, can be destructive of writing: we all recall Jane Austen's years of silence when her father had to give up his house and take the family into lodgings; we remember Sylvia Plath's hectic early-morning sleepless composition before her babies awoke; and there are doubtless other examples. A writer who persists, phase after phase, usually has some intrinsic and compelling self and style demanding expression. If we try to isolate the self and style which appeared in *A Change of World* and which have continued, through age and variation, all the way up to *Diving into the Wreck,* we are asking, really, which are Rich's best poems, how her voice makes itself both remarkable and beautiful.

Rich hit her stride, and wrote her first "perfect" poem (of her voice at that time) in her second volume, *The Diamond Cutters* (1955). The poem in question, "The Middle-Aged," is one of a distinguished group, including "The Tourist and the Town," "Lucifer in the Train," "The Wild Sky," "Villa Adriana," and "Landscape of the Star," which all, in some way, deal with homelessness; and that homelessness, with its accompanying ache of filial nostalgia, is the new theme, coming into the ascendant, which distinctly marks *The Diamond-Cutters* as an advance over the first volume. Sometimes the pain of departure and separation is overt and unmediated:

> Imperceptibly
> That landscape altered; now in paler air
> Tree, hill and rock stood out resigned, severe,
> Beside the strangled field, the stream run dry.
> ("Lucifer in the Train")

* * *

The shape of *The Diamond Cutters* suggests that Rich may need to write explicit *cris du coeur* as sketches, so to speak, for a more contained and disciplined later poem. It is odd that some readers will so placidly receive and even praise such unmediated cries of filial longing, but will become irrationally damning about a single cry of unmediated anger. These hysterias only prove that Rich is touching intense and widely diffused feelings; a poet could hardly ask for more. In her poems, Rich sees more deeply than in her recent prose propaganda; poetry makes her more reflective and more self-corrective, less inflexible, more pained.

In *Snapshots of a Daughter-in-Law* (1963), we find that marriage has turned the earlier filial exile-in-space into something considerably more bitter—separation under the same roof, a sense of separate-and-not-equal lives bequeathed to men and women, with women's only claim that of a more arcane insight into Nature:

> . . . has Nature shown
> her household books to you, daughter-in-law,
> that her sons never saw?

The silent isolation of minds in marriage is followed by a choking, deprived speech. The central poem in this volume is without doubt "A Marriage in the 'Sixties," a poem still hoping for the best and yet unwilling to dissemble the worst.[3] "My words," says Rich, watching those words drop unheard and neglected, "reach you as through a telephone/ where some submarine echo of my voice/ blurts knowledge you can't use." ("The Lag"). In this volume, Rich's lines loosen up into free verse; we may assume various influences, from Eliot to Lowell to Plath, but since the modern movement as a whole was on its way toward dispensing with rhyme, it was inevitable that Rich should forsake her sweetness, cadence, and stanzas once her life began to refuse its earlier arrangements. Nervous, hardened, noting harshly that only cutting onions can provoke her unwept tears into her eyes, she moves under a "load of unexpired purpose, which drains/ slowly." Rich's effects now depend only on metaphor, juxta-position, and adroit lineation; she vomits up "dead gobbets" of herself, "abortive, murdered, or never willed" for new recognition; she

---

3. In the original essay, lines of "A Marriage in the 'Sixties" were quoted; in this volume the poem appears on pp. 18–19.

crawls out of her cocoon like a fish attempting the grand evolution-
ary trick of becoming a bird.[4]

If, as Rich's early pattern suggests, blunter poems are followed
by subtler ones, *Necessities of Life* derives its power from its absorp-
tion of all past phases into its present one. In "Autumn Sequence,"
Rich forces herself to that generosity toward past selves:

> Generosity is drying out,
>
> it's an act of will to remember
> May's sticky-mouthed buds
> on the provoked magnolias.

But that act of will makes this volume almost an obituary; at least
it is the obituary of a whole section of life. The title poem—a second
talisman, at least for me, to join with "The Middle-Aged," shows
a new self emerging and seeking a new place in the world:

> Piece by piece I seem
> to re-enter the world: I first began
>
> a small, fixed dot, still see
> that old myself, a dark-blue thumbtack
>
> pushed into the scene,
> a hard little head protruding
>
> from the pointillist's buzz and bloom.

We cannot help noticing how free from compulsion Rich's images
have become. The early poems were so neat in their useful skeins
of imagery; if a color appeared in the upper left of the tapestry,
it was sure to reappear, economically but predictably, in the lower
right. Now precision of feeling and exactness of recollection govern
the correlative, and though the visual reference apparent in the
thumbtack and the pointillist is maintained, it is allowed consider-
able freedom. In adolescence come passion and ambition, melting
the pigments:

> After a time the dot
>
> begins to ooze. Certain heats
> melt it.
>   Now I was hurriedly
>
> blurring into ranges
> of burnt red, burning green,
>
> whole biographies swam up and
> swallowed me like Jonah.

---

4. In the original essay, "Ghost of a Chance" was quoted in full; in this volume it
appears on p. 20.

> Jonah! I was Wittgenstein,
> Mary Wollstonecraft, the soul
>
> of Louis Jouvet, dead
> in a blown-up photograph.

There is a hiatus in the poem at this point, as though the self-devouring of adolescence were nameable, but the other-devouring of marriage and child-rearing were not. The "hard little head" become photograph loses its painterly dimension and becomes a dry bulb waiting out its time of deprivation, "gone underground" like Herbert's flower, through "all the hard weather":

> Till, wolfed almost to shreds,
> I learned to make myself
>
> unappetizing. Scaly as a dry bulb
> thrown into a cellar
>
> I used myself, let nothing use me.
> Like being on a private dole
>
> Sometimes more like kneading bricks in Egypt.

In this poverty of slavery—and the comparisons tell us that even the "privileged" life of a Cambridge wife and mother can feel like that—the poem reaches its central minimal state in an exhausted miserliness keeping others at bay:

> What life was there, was mine,
>
> now and again to lay
> one hand on a warm brick
>
> and touch the sun's ghost
> with economical joy,
>
> now and again to name
> over the bare necessities.

This beautiful passage, though it could perhaps not have been written before Stevens' poetry of poverty, has the touch of the physical in it that Stevens' poetry lacked: that warm brick and its ghostly heat did not inhabit Stevens' universe. Those "certain heats" of adolescence have dwindled to this spectral form: passion and ambition alike almost expire in this daily kneading of the bricks, this being "wolfed almost to shreds" by others. But the devouring demand has, with time, eased; a tentative green shoot rises from the root cellar; "Who would have thought my shrivel'd heart/ Could have recover'd greennesse?" asks Herbert under similar conditions. But Rich's resurrection is not Herbert's cyclical one; she will never again be a flower. However, she can be a cabbage, an eel, something sturdy and slippery at once (and female and male at once, the androgynous imagery suggests):

> So much for those days. Soon
> practice may make me middling perfect, I'll
>
> dare inhabit the world
> trenchant in motion as an eel, solid
>
> as a cabbage-head. I have invitations:
> a curl of mist steams upward
>
> from a field, visible as my breath.

Encouraging, brisk lines: they tell what every depleted mother must feel when the haze and stumbling of physical and psychic tiredness finally lift after a decade of babies. But where is the new society to join, when child-bearing is over? Where but among the old wives?

> houses along a road stand waiting
>
> like old women knitting, breathless
> to tell their tales.

In these lines, acquiescence and rebellion compete: that the little dark-blue thumbtack should come to this; that the girl who dreamed of being Wittgenstein should join the garrulous crones. And yet, what else can the normal lot be; given the submission of the soul in all those years of Egyptian bondage, given the confines of the root-cellar, is it not enough to sit on the doorstep and knit?

That was as far ahead as Rich could see in 1962, and, as always, she told us life as she saw it. It is with an almost desperate vertigo that we come from this poem and others like it to the poems of violent change in the later books, when Rich feels picked up and thrown by life into jangling new positions, unforeseen, unasked-for but welcomed as they come. The more reproachful of her critics have assumed that her revolutionary stances are chosen and therefore blameworthy; I see them rather as part of the inexplicable ongoingness of life, to be reported like the rest. Better a change than the falsely "mature" acceptance of the unacceptable, a stance that Rich falls into off and on in *Necessities of Life,* notably in the increasingly expedient "literariness" of the poem "After Dark" on her father's death, and in the forced ending of the fine poem "Like This Together," where Rich declares that love can be kept alive by our working at it, that the dry scaly bulb can be pried into life.[5]

* * *

The two books preceding *Diving into the Wreck* are waiting out some murky transition: the most explicit poem in *Leaflets* (1969) jettisons every past except the residual animal instinct of self-

---

5. In the original essay, "Like This Together, 5" was quoted in full; in this volume it appears on pp. 27–28.

preservation, and every future except death; comparing herself to "the red fox, the vixen" and denying any connection to the ascetic New England settlers (like the Israelites, a "chosen people") with their "instinct mortified in a virgin forest," Rich says:

> what does she want
> with the dreams of dead vixens,
> the apotheosis of Reynard,
> the literature of fox-hunting?
> Only in her nerves the past
> sings, a thrill of self-preservation. . . .
> and she springs toward her den
> every hair on her pelt alive
> with tidings of the immaculate present. . . .
> She has no archives,
> no heirlooms, no future
> except death
> and I could be more
> her sister than theirs
> who chopped their way across these hills
> —a chosen people.
>
> ("Abnegation")

This vixen ("wise-looking in a sexy way" in Rich's unfortunate description) has none of the vitality of torn-down Cambridge, and so is allegorical rather than convincingly metaphorical, but this rather weak poem makes the clear point of the book; jettison the past, live in sex and the present, forget the mind, tradition, and sublimation.

* * *

[In *The Will to Change,* in a poem called "Shooting Script,"] Rich has abandoned the sentimental fantasy of being a purely animal vixen, but she still wishes for a hypothesized primitive physical human self, like the villagers whose ancestors made the pots:

Of simple choice they are the villagers; their clothes come with them like red clay roads they have been walking.

The sole of the foot is a map, the palm of the hand a letter, learned by heart and worn close to the body.

In the new primitivism, the poet must abandon his magic lantern and give up "the temptations of the projector": but in fact the projector itself had come to grief, refusing to move on to the next slide, projecting one image "over & over on empty walls." One must "see instead the web of cracks filtering across the plaster":

initial split, the filaments thrown out from that impasse.
To read there the map of the future, the roads radiating from the

To reread the instructions on your palm; to find there how the lifeline, broken, keeps its direction.

To read the etched rays of the bullet-hole left years ago in the
glass; to know in every direction of the light what fracture is.
("Shooting Script," number 14)

Giving up the prism, the lens, the map, and pulling herself up by
her own roots, Rich, as *The Will to Change* closes, eats the last meal
in her own neighborhood and prepares, deprived of all instruments,
to move on, guided only by the fortuitous cracks in the plaster, the
innate lifeline, the traumatic rays of the bullet-hole. She could hardly
have been more frank; from formalism to—not freedom, but, as
always—a new version of truth. If this is a revolution, it is one
bound like Ixion on the wheel of the past—environmental past in
the plaster, genetic past in the lifeline, traumatic past in the bullet-
hole. And if it is revolution, it is one which does not wish to deny
the reality of past choices and past modes of life. Putting off in
her boat, Rich watches "the lights on the shore I had left for a long
time; each one, it seemed to me, was a light I might have lit, in the
old days" ("Shooting Script," II, number 13). Houselights and
hearthfires, abandoned, remembered, light the departure.

And so, in *Diving into the Wreck,* the old questions are still min-
ing like moles underneath: tradition, civilization, the mind and the
body, woman, man, love, writing—and the war added as a metaphor,
so far as I can see, for illustration of the war between the sexes
rather than for especially political commentary. In the most medita-
tive and searching poem (besides the title poem) in *Diving into the
Wreck,*[5] Rich forsakes distinctions between men and women, for the
most part, and sees us all as crippled creatures, scarred by that
process of socialization and nurture which had been, when she began
writing, her possession, her treasure; tapestries, Europe, recorders,
Bach—the whole edifice of civilization, of which she now sees the
dark side—war, exploitation, and deadening of instinct.

*   *   *

The forcefulness of *Diving into the Wreck* comes from the wish
not to huddle wounded, but to explore the caverns, the scars, the
depths of the wreckage. At first these explorations must reactivate
all the old wounds, inflame all the scar tissue, awaken all the sup-
pressed anger, and inactivate the old language invented for dealing
with the older self. But I find no betrayal of continuity in these later
books, only courage in the refusal to write in forms felt to be out-
grown. I hope that the curve into more complex expression visible
in her earlier books will recur as Rich continues to publish, and that
these dispatches from the battlefield will be assimilated into a more
complete poetry. Given Rich's precocious and sustained gifts, I see
no reason to doubt her future. The title poem that closed *The Dia-*

5. "Meditations for a Savage Child."

mond Cutters says that the poetic supply is endless: after one dia-
mond has been cut, "Africa/ Will yield you more to do." When
new books follow, these most recent poems will I think be seen as
the transition to a new generosity and a new self-forgetfulness.

ERICA JONG

Visionary Anger †

* * *

The line of development from "Living in Sin" to *Diving into the
Wreck* is a serpentine line, yet there has never been any question
where Adrienne Rich is going. Along the way, there have been
great numbers of extraordinary poems that never flinched from
dealing with sexuality, hunger, motherhood, loneliness, blood and
revolution in both the personal and the public sense. If you read
Diving into the Wreck and then go back and consider the books be-
fore it (*A Change of World, The Diamond Cutters, Snapshots of a
Daughter-in-Law, Necessities of Life, Leaflets,* and *The Will to
Change*), I think you will see that one of Adrienne Rich's most re-
current themes has always been the relationship between poetry and
patriarchy.

Poetry and patriarchy. The problems of woman in a patriarchal
society. That is, in part, what *Diving into the Wreck* is about. Yet
it is not about patriarchy in a narrowly political sense. Rich is one
of very few poets who can deal with political issues in her poems
without letting them degenerate into socialist realism, because her
notion of politics is not superficial; it is essentially psychological and
organic. We all give lip-service to this concept of politics, yet few
of us truly understand it. We all claim to believe that political op-
pression and personal feelings are related, and yet a great deal of
the self-consciously polemical poetry that has come out of the
Women's Movement reads like a generalized rant and it lacks any
sort of psychological grounding. The poet has not really looked into
herself and told it true. She has been content to echo simplistic
slogans.

Adrienne Rich's concept of patriarchy has nothing simplistic
about it. Her feminism is a natural extension of her poetry because,
for her, feminism *means* empathy. And empathy is the essential
tool of the poet. It is akin to the quality Keats called "negative capa-
bility"—that unique gift for projecting oneself into other states of

† From *Ms.*, II, 1 (July, 1973), 31–33. Reprinted by permission of the author.

consciousness. If Rich sees the role of the poet and the role of the revolutionary as totally compatible, it is because she understands that the most profound revolutons will come from the development of our capacity for empathy.

In a brilliant essay entitled "The Anti-Feminist Woman," she summed this up in these words: "I believe that feminism must imply an imaginative identification with all women (and with the ghostly woman in all men) and that the feminist must, because she can, extend this act of the imagination as far as possible."

The phrase "the ghostly woman in all men" is crucial. Rich is alarmed not only by the outward signs of discrimination against women in our patriarchal culture, but also by the way this culture suppresses the nurturant qualities in men, in children, and in societal institutions. She is a feminist because she feels "endangered, psychically and physically, by this society, and because [she believes] we have come to an edge of history when men—insofar as they are embodiments of the patriarchal idea—have become dangerous to children and other living things, themselves included." Her feminism is far more radical and far-reaching than equal-pay-for-equal-work or the establishment of fifty-fifty marriages. It envisions a world in which empathy, mothering, "a concern for the quality of life," "a connection with the natural and the extrasensory order" will not be relegated to women (who then have no power to implement these concerns on a practical level), but will be encouraged in the society at large.

So she is not talking only about discrimination against women, but about discrimination against the *feminine*.

(By the *feminine* I mean the nurturant qualities in all people—whatever their sex. I realize that the term is unsatisfactory and reflex the sexism of our language. The real nature of the feminine and the masculine can never be ascertained until we have a truly equitable social order. Adrienne Rich, however, does seem to be convinced that the feminine principle is more nurturant and the masculine more competitive. I think she might also agree that this need not *always* be so. But her main point seems to be that after too many centuries of uncontested phallic power, we need to right the balance. Women may have to take over for a while to save men from their own self-destructiveness. Eventually, though, Rich would probably hope for a world in which men and women could work together in harmony.)

* * *

Again and again the dead end of male civilization is dramatized in these poems:

> A man's world. But finished.
> They themselves have sold it to the machines.

Or:

> A man is asleep in the next room
> He has spent a whole day
> standing, throwing stones into the black pool
> which keeps its blackness.

Or:

> His mind is too simple, I cannot go on
> sharing his nightmares.

But the poems are not only about dead ends. They are about loneliness and the various forms it takes: the loneliness of being a woman in a male-dominated culture, the loneliness of being a life-giver in a world that is in love with death, the loneliness of being an artist, an outsider, a survivor. Human loneliness is one of the great themes in all the arts, and Adrienne Rich depicts it more intensely here than in any other recent book I know. But she also shows that loneliness can be the beginning of rebirth. The woman, because she stands outside the death-dealing culture and its power games, can be a visionary who points the way to redemption. And these poems are also very much about redemption: about sister giving birth to sister, and woman giving birth to herself. For instance, in "The Mirror in Which Two Are Seen as One":

> your mother dead and you unborn
> your two hands grasping your head
> drawing it down against the blade of life
> your nerves the nerves of a midwife
> learning her trade

The speaker of this book is a survivor. She has all the pain of the survivor, but she also has the survivor's unique vision. The subterranean life of the book, which flows through its images, is full of scars, faults, stains, deserts, leaking blood, rotting logs, ruined cities, and wrecked ships. The survivor-poet dives into this wreckage and tries to salvage meaning and a new life. She must give birth to herself and to her sisters, and she must also try to save man from himself—though she spends her own life energy endlessly in trying: "The waste of my love goes on this way/trying to save you from yourself."

If I've made this sound as though the speaker of these poems is a sort of Wonder Woman determined to rescue the world by heroic feats, then I've misled you. Rich *does* imply that women are strong and must learn to be even stronger (which is one of the glorious things about her book—especially after reading all those so-called feminist novels in which women are depicted as helpless victims); but the speaker of these poems need not be seen exclusively as a woman, even as a Wonder Woman. She could be *any* outsider, any person who is alienated from our destructive culture, any life-giver (female or male) who wishes to raise a voice against death-worship and the waste of love.

In fact, some of the most interesting poems in the book are those in which Rich imagines an androgynous creature who tran- scends conventional maleness and conventional femaleness and walks through the city like a stranger—*my visionary anger cleansing my sight/ and the detailed perceptions of mercy/ flowering from that anger:*

> I am the androgyne
> I am the living mind you fail to describe
> in your dead language
> the lost noun, the verb surviving
> only in the infinitive
> the letters of my name are written under the lids
> of the newborn child
>
> ("The Stranger")

In "Diving into the Wreck," the title poem, it is the androgyne who dives into the wreck *to see the damage that was done/ and the treasures that prevail.*

> And I am here, the mermaid whose dark hair
> streams black, the merman in his armored body
> We circle silently
> about the wreck
> we dive into the hold.
> I am she: I am he
> whose drowned face sleeps with open eyes

This stranger-poet-survivor carries "a book of myths" in which her/his "names do not appear." These are the old myths of patri- archy, the myths that split male and female irreconcilably into two warring factions, the myths that perpetuate the battle between the sexes. Implicit in Rich's image of the androgyne is the idea that we must write new myths, create new definitions of humanity which will not glorify this angry chasm but heal it. Rich's visionary andro- gyne reminds me of Virginia Woolf's assertion that the great artist must be mentally bisexual. But Rich takes this idea even further: it is not only the artist who must make the emphatic leap beyond gender, but *any* of us who would try to save the world from de- struction.

* * *

WENDY MARTIN

From Patriarchy to the Female Principle: A Chronological Reading of Adrienne Rich's Poems

Adrienne Rich's poetry records her struggle to create a strong independent self capable of demanding and sustaining egalitarian relationships and documents her efforts to create a new social and political vision. In addition to reaching out to other contemporary women, the mother, sister, and friend, the philosopher and prostitute, Rich's poetry reaches back in time to such women as Caroline Herschel, George Eliot, Virginia Woolf and Mary Wollstonecraft, who resisted the constraints on their situation; and she looks forward to the emergence of the new woman—a future heroine who will be in full command of her energy and power:

> Well,
> she's long about her coming, who must be
> more merciless to herself than history.
> Her mind full to the wind, I see her plunge
> breasted and glancing through the currents,
> taking the light upon her
> at least as beautiful as any boy
> or helicopter
> ("Snapshots of a Daughter-in-Law")

Historical continuity with those who began to explore the potentialities of a fuller and freer womanhood sustains women now in the search for identity and community in the future. A chronological reading of Rich's poems will trace out, in her discovery of a female principle beyond the patriarchal definitions of woman, the evolving consciousness of the modern woman.

In her elaboration of the future heroine, Rich echoes Simone de Beauvoir's description of the woman of a new age: "She comes down from the remoteness of ages, from Thebes, from Crete, from Chichén-Itzá; and she is also the totem set deep in the African jungle; she is a helicopter and she is a bird; and there is this, the greatest wonder of all: under her tinted hair the forest murmur becomes a thought, and words issue from her breasts."[1] She is the heiress of the ancient goddesses, the child of the furies, sharing their knowledge of the mysteries of blood and birth; yet, resilient and articulate, she ushers in the future. Like a helicopter, she is able

---

1. Simone de Beauvoir, *The Second Sex,* tr. H. M. Parshley (New York, 1953), p. 729 [*Martin's note*].

to land and take off in precarious places, rescuing people who are in trouble. For both Rich and de Beauvoir, modern civilization needs the vision of such powerful women in order to survive.

Snapshots of a Daughter-in-Law (1954–1962) focuses, as the title suggests, on the experience of a woman whose identity is based, to a large extent, on her legal and economic responsibilities to men. She is alone and alienated from other women, and her life consists of attending to the duties and rituals of the household. While outwardly conforming to the domestic scenario, she broods about the stunted growth of both women and men in patriarchal society in which the mind rules the body and eros has been sacrificed to civilization. Most of her energy is devoted to sustaining and nurturing men, yet she manages to survive in a culture which trivializes her contributions and does not honor her needs.

The daughter-in-law experiences conflict between the demands of others and the demands of the self. She takes care of household details, even if with the grim determination of preparing for a funeral: "Soon we'll be off. I'll pack us into parcels,/ stuff us in barrels, shroud us in newspapers,/ pausing to marvel at old bargain sales" ("Passing On," 1959); but her imagination will not let her retreat into a world of packing and shopping. "You are no dream, old genius./ I smell you, get my teeth on edge,/ stand in my sweat— in mercury—even as you prime your feathers and set sail" ("The Raven," 1959).

In *A Room of One's Own*, Virginia Woolf writes that in order for women to free their creative energies, they must learn "to kill the angel in the house," to cease to be ministering and self-sacrificing. While it is essential for all people to strive to be responsive, loving, concerned human beings, it is very destructive for women to be expected to give priority to the needs of others; to serve men, or even children, in the name of compassion can be damaging. Femininity based on self-denial is masochism, but self-sacrifice is a cultural norm for women.[2]

"Snapshots of a Daughter-in-Law" (1958–1960), the title poem, explores the female heritage of dissipated energy, dependency, and self-hate. The poem chronicles the fragmented lives of women who live vicariously through men, who are excessively preoccupied with romantic love and crippled by their emotional and economic dependency on men: "Our blight has been our sinecure:/ mere talent was enough for us—/ glitter in fragments and rough drafts." The poem reflects the 1950's, when the "feminine mystique," the twentieth-century counterpart to the nineteenth-century cult of true

2. For an excellent discussion of masochism as the basis for traditional femininity, see Karen Horney, *Feminine Psychology* (New York: W. W. Norton, 1967) [*Martin's note*].

womanhood, was the accepted norm for women.[3] The "true woman" is compliant and ornamental, "sweetly laughing, sweetly singing"; her legs are shaved and gleaming, her hair falls softly over her cheek, and her silk skirt is arranged seductively against her knees. She constantly looks to men for approval; she has no core of self and values herself according to her ability to please men—if she is not charming and alluring, she has failed.

Rich laments the mediocrity, self-indulgence, lack of will and discipline that results from the feminine mystique. She mourns the waste of the enormous energies of women "in the prime of [their] life" in a culture which esteems women for their ornamental beauty but not for their experience and wisdom. The woman who is no longer young and seductive has lost what little power she has in patriarchal society—"the drained and flagging bosom of our middle years." Here is no community of women, no belief or confidence in the power of sisterhood. Female energy is turned inward manifesting itself as guilt, anxiety, or hysteria, anger spirals into depression, self-hate and even madness and suicide: "A thinking woman sleeps with monsters./ The beak that grips her, she becomes." [4]

Margaret Fuller wrote at length in *Woman in the Nineteenth Century,* her feminist tract published in 1844, about the necessity for women to participate in the larger arena of life: "Women, self-centered, would never be absorbed by any relation; it would only be an experience to her as to a man. It is a vulgar error that love, *a* love, to women is her whole existence; she is also born for Truth and Love in their universal energy." But the "true woman" has an addiction to romantic love—her mission is to attract and hold her man.

Rich prefaces section 7 of "Snapshots of a Daughter-in-Law" with a quotation from Mary Wollstonecraft's *Thoughts on the Education of Daughters* (1787) in which Wollstonecraft insists on the primacy of her own perceptions; not content to see her reflection in a man's eyes nor willing to accept male definitions of reality, she demands that women must be educated in order to be able to take responsibility for their own lives. However, those women such as Wollstonecraft and Fuller who do attempt to be self-determining are "labelled harpy, shrew, and whore." [5] Historically, feminism represents the

3. See Barbara Welter, "The Cult of True Womanhood," in *The American Sisterhood: Writings of the Feminist Movement from the Colonial Times to the Present,* ed. Wendy Martin (New York: Harper & Row, 1972), pp. 244–256 [*Martin's note*].
4. See Phyllis Chesler, *Woman and Madness* (Garden City, N.Y.: Doubleday, 1972) for an analysis and documentation of the relationship between the repression of female aggression and anger, and severe depression and suicide [*Martin's note*].
5. For a discussion of the systematic repression of female sexuality and intellectual independence, see Mary Jane Sherfey, *The Nature and Evolution of Female Sexuality* (Random House, 1972), and Wendy Martin, "Seduced and Abandoned in the New World: The Fallen Woman in American Fiction," in *The American Sisterhood,* pp. 258–272 [*Martin's note*].

efforts of women to participate in the cultural dialogue which shapes reality—patriarchy represents the monopoly of this political and social process by men.[6]

The formula that defines women as private beings—as homemakers—and men as public persons—bread-winners—is damaging to men as well as to women. In "The Knight" (1957), Rich asks "who will unhorse this rider/ and free him from between/ the walls of iron, the emblems/ crushing his chest with their weight?" To a large extent, a man in patriarchal society is valued according to his financial assets; most often it is the powerful, wealthy man who is defined as attractive—eros and money are intertwined for many women. In order to gain economic mastery, a man must repress sensitivity, tenderness, and intuition, thereby denying or repressing many of his most basic emotions. If women become stronger, learn to take care of themselves, share equally in the responsibility for survival, it may then be possible for the knight to remove the armor which shields him from feeling. The pragmatic basis for relationships which defines men as providers and protectors and makes economic captives of women must shift to a more genuinely emotionally satisfying context.

The poems written in the second half of *Snapshots of a Daughter-in-Law* (1960–1962) reveal an increasing impatience with this divided world of men and women. The poet insists on understanding who she is, what her responses are to a given historical context: "Since I was more than a child/ trying on a thousand faces/ I have wanted one thing: to know simply as I know my name/ at any given moment, where I stand" ("Double Monologue," 1960). In "Readings of History" (1960), Rich scans the past to understand the present better and attempts to locate herself in the historical flux. She realizes that the social order of the nineteenth century, based on the ideology of the monogamous couple bound to each

6. In general, the exclusion of women from public life has become much more pronounced in western Europe and America since the Industrial Revolution. In colonial America, women did the same work as men because there was a shortage of labor; in addition to bearing many children, they supervised "the production, processing, and preparation of food; they butchered animals, made textiles, and acted as physicians, midwives, and nurses. Women operated printing presses, were owners of general stores and bookstores, were proprietresses of taverns; women were accomplished in glass, metal, wood, and leather crafts. Women were shippers as well as bakers, and there were even a few women blacksmiths. Women were also lawyers, morticians, owners of saw mills, flour mills, and cider mills." (For a more elaborate discussion see the Introduction to *The American Sisterhood*, pp. 3–6.) Since the need for labor was somewhat diminished by the Industrial Revolution, middle-class women were encouraged to remain at home to nurture their children and to provide a haven for their husbands. The isolation of women in private dwellings, then, has taken place in the last century; besides, the nuclear family itself is a relatively recent historical phenomenon, as is demonstrated by Phillipe Ariés, *Centuries of Childhood: A Social History of Family Life* (New York: Alfred A. Knopf, 1962) [*Martin's note*].

other by a complex web of necessity and cooperation, has changed: "I knew beyond all doubt how dead that couple was." She contemplates the struggle of others to define the self, to create meaning in a rapidly shifting world; reflecting on the lives of Pirandello, her great-grand-uncle who fought in the Civil War, the Victorians, the women of World War II, of contemporary women whose "nylon luggage matches/ eyelids/ expertly azured," she understands that her life is also part of a larger historical context: "I, too, have lived in history."

Rich commits herself to change in spite of the risks involved in having no preconceived idea of where she is going. In "Prospective Immigrants Please Note" (1962), she prepares to take a journey in uncharted territory, opens the door to the future, knowing "The door itself/ makes no promises. It is only a door." The opening of the door is extremely important because it marks a fundamental change in her way of approaching experience. It signals her willingness to take risks, to experience conflict and acute anxiety, to tolerate ambiguity and to perceive her life as being open-ended: "Things look at you doubly/ and you must look back/ and let them happen." Essentially the poet is committing herself to living in the present—to process. Since the past does not provide traditions which are viable for the modern woman, she must discover the meaning of her life for herself.

In *Necessities of Life* (1962–1965), Rich pares away the layers of social conditioning, ritualized roles and programmed responses in order to locate the core of self, the essentials of her existence. In the title poem, she again expresses feelings of being consumed by past lives. Wittgenstein's analytic scrutiny of language, Wollstonecraft's intellectual independence, Louis Jouvet's creativity as a film director make claims on her imagination and emotional energy: "Whole biographies swam up and/ swallowed me like Jonah." Retreating from history, she severs all connections to the past in order to claim her own life: "I used myself, let nothing use me. . . . What life was there, was mine." Not until the poet separates herself from a larger social and historical context is she able to determine her personal reality. This process of separation is an essential phase of identity formation for the oppressed feminists as well as third world peoples.

In addition to attempting to determine the essentials of her private reality, Rich turns to nature to learn what she can about the fundamental characteristics of life. She does not permit herself the romantic indulgence of using nature as "ego's arcady," as a screen on which to project the self; instead, she is able to transcend the dichotomy of mind and matter, becoming aware of the connection of all living things:

> . . . my soul wheeled back
> and burst into my body.
>
> Found! ready or not.
> If I move now, the sun
> naked between the trees
> will melt me as I lie.
> ("In the Woods," 1963)

Nature is more than a pastoral idyll, it teaches basic lessons of life. The sun, for example, as a source of primal energy can give us necessary if disquieting truths about ourselves:

> Is it in the sun that truth begins?
> Lying under that battering light
> the first few hours of summer
> I felt scraped clean, washed down
> to ignorance.
> ("The Corpse-Plant," 1963)

Erotic love is one of the few experiences in modern life which reconnects us with our senses and biological rhythms: "Because of you I notice/ the taste of water,/ a luxury I might/ otherwise have missed" ("Like This Together," 1963). Eros suffuses her world making it radiant and is an antidote to the "aloof, selective stare," the "otherness that affronts us" from the man who is dedicated to the primacy of his mind.

The destructive effect of separation of the mind and body, spirit and matter, is one of the major themes in Adrienne Rich's poetry, and she perceives this impoverishment of life to be related to the patriarchal need for mastery; the plenitude of nature is ignored by men who must be dominant:

> Your flag is dried-blood, turkey comb
> flayed stiff in the wind. . . .
> Your eye blurs in a wet smoke.
> the stubble freezes under your heel
> ("Autumn Sequence," 1964)

There is no connection, no harmonious balance between man and nature—he is alienated from nature even while in it.

Urban civilization is composed of monuments to male dominance, to the principle of mind over matter:

> Over him, over you, a great roof is rising,
> a great wall: no temporary shelter.
> Did you tell yourself these beams would melt,
>
> these fiery blocs dissolve?
> Did you choose to build this thing?

> Have you stepped back to see what it is?
> ("Spring Thunder," 1965)

The poet distances herself from these patriarchal landscapes and returns again to her own experience with an awareness that her culture does not reflect her concerns and, in fact, could destroy her:

> I am gliding backward away from those who knew me
> as the moon grows thinner and finally shuts its lantern.
> I can be replaced a thousand times,
> a box containing death.
> When you put out your hand to touch me
> you are already reaching toward an empty space.
> ("Moth Hour," 1965)

Leaflets (1965–1968) begins with the poet's retreat into privatism and ends with political rage. In this volume, the poet merges personal and public realities; the disappointments and failures of romantic love, the limits of individualism, the lack of reverence for life, the cruelty of war, a growing consciousness of the community of women, an increasing desire to create a meaningful world through poetry, through revolutionary politics, are all interconnected. Rich no longer distinguishes her private miseries from public failures. Although she experiences rage about being a victim of history and about having to live in a world she didn't create, she discovers that the personal and political cannot be separated, that her life is part of a larger social fabric. She also discovers that changing her personal life has political implications. The poems in *Leaflets* explore possibilities for transformations of lives—private and public.

Rich thereby transcends the traditional dichotomy between art and life, aesthetics and politics. She is writing poetry with the intention to change people's lives: "I wanted to choose words that even you/ would have to be changed by" ("Implosions," 1968).

Determined to have a political impact, she is willing to risk experiencing considerable pain, if necessary, rather than to accept the rules of a deadening society:

> I'd rather
> taste blood, yours or mine, flowing
> from a sudden slash, than cut all day
> with blunt scissors on dotted lines
> like the teacher told.
> ("On Edges," 1968)

The pain, however, is mutually shared, the result of trying to confront experience directly.

In her effort to create a new life, Rich establishes a fundamental connection between herself and all people—hurt and destruction to others is hurt and destruction to herself:

In the bed the pieces fly together
and the rifts fill   or else
my body is a list   of wounds
symmetrically placed
a village
blown open   by planes
that did not   finish the job
                    ("Nightbreak," 1968)

No longer is she an isolated individual but part of the human family, and her identification with oppressed peoples is intensified.

Rich's poem "To Frantz Fanon" (1968), psychiatrist and revolutinary who lived in Algeria, reveals her involvement in the revolutionary community. Insisting that it is important for oppressed people to fight back in order to gain selfhood and identity, Fanon encouraged the Algerians to resist the indoctrination of the French. Rich thinks of Fanon as a schoolboy:

What I see best is the length
of your fingers
pressing the pencil
into the barred page

of the French child's-copybook
with its Cartesian squares its grilled
trap of holy geometry
where your night-sweats streamed out
in language

The Algerians were systematically taught by the French to ignore their own culture and instead to learn such useless facts as the distance from the Arch de Triomphe to the Place de Concorde. This pattern of socialization parallels the training of women to assume supportive but subordinate roles in patriarchal society.

"Leaflets" (1968), the title poem, reflects the political ferment of the late sixties, when there was widespread protest over the war in Viet Nam, and a major upheaval in France. Rich is part of this political ferment, "life without caution/ the only worth living" and is surprised by her ability to sustain the stress which is an inevitable part of rapid political change. To illustrate, she quotes these lines from Chekhov's journal, written in 1890 during his trip to the penal colony at Sakhalin: *"that I can live half a year/ as I have never lived up to this time—."* Recognizing that this period of political change is one of dislocation not only for herself but for the revolutionary male, "Your face/ stretched like a mask/ begins to tear/ as you speak of Che Guevara/ Bolivia, Nanterre."

Although she often becomes tangled in his words, she feels deep empathy for the revolutionary male, and she acknowledges the importance of their common struggle: "We're fighting for a slash of recognition." Later, she will pull away from his influence just as the women who were political activists in the sixties realized it was necessary to determine their own political vision because radical men were frequently as sexist as traditional patriarchs.[7]

In *The Will to Change* (1968–1970), Rich continues to probe the failures of a culture based on greed and repression which denies the basic needs of most of its population—women, children, the aged, Blacks, Mexicans, Indians—and all other people who are not part of the patriarchal elite. The poet is "a woman in the prime of life, with certain powers/ and those powers severely limited by authorities whose faces I rarely see. . . . a woman feeling the fullness of her powers/ at the precise moment when she must not use them/ a woman sworn to lucidity" ("I Dream I'm the Death of Orpheus," 1968).

Not only does sexist society fail to acknowledge the strength of women, it prevents women from understanding their own experiences as well as their power. Although Rich articulates her experiences with depth and honesty, she must struggle to come to terms with her own experience as a modern woman because even the very language she must use is not her own: "This is the oppressor's language/ yet I need it to talk to you" ("The Burning of Paper Instead of Children," 1968).

Since language shapes reality,[8] Rich is confined by the "oppressor's language" which makes it difficult for her to understand and assert the validity of her experience. The definition and articulation of her reality require not only the will to change but considerable discipline and courage; sometimes she despairs about the failures of communication and wonders how to create a reality which would connect her to others: "The fracture of order/ the repair of speech/ to overcome this suffering."

Rich continues to explore the loss of connection between mind and body searching for the possibilities for overcoming these dichotomies. Again, erotic love creates possibilities for fusion of spirit and matter, and she writes of lovers communicating in their dreams when the barriers of the ego are let down: "Talk to me with your body through my dreams/ Tell me what we are going through" ("The Blue Ghazals"). Wondering when eros will suffuse our lives, when the breach between mind and spirit will be healed, Rich asks, "When will we lie clearheaded in our flesh again/ with the cold edge of night driving us close together?"

7. See Robin Morgan, "Goodbye to All That," *RAT: Subterranean News,* Vol. 2, no. 27 (February 6, 1970), 1–6. Reprinted in *The American Sisterhood,* pp. 360–367 [*Martin's note*].
8. See the following for a discussion of the relationship of language to social reality: Peter Berger and Thomas Luckmann, *The Social Construction of Real-*ity: *A Treatise in the Sociology of Knowledge* (Garden City, N.Y.: Doubleday, 1966); Edward Sapir, *Culture, Language and Personality* (Berkeley: University of California Press, 1966); Benjamin Lee Whorf, *Language, Thought and Reality* (Cambridge, Mass.: Technological Press of M.I.T., 1956) [*Martin's note*].

The reclamation of feeling in this context of emotional sterility and repressed sexuality is a revolutionary act: *"The moment when a feeling enters the body/ is political. This touch is political."* Feeling is political because it indicates an awareness of and responsiveness to the world in which one lives—feeling, then, can guide us in the reconstruction of our lives. In part, this is what "power to the people means"—a recognition that the emotional and physical energy of many people should not be controlled by a few individuals for profit, that a society should meet the needs of its members.[9]

In *Diving into the Wreck* (1971–1972) Rich asserts that the creation of a community of women is the necessary antidote to the excesses of individualism. Hoping that the nurturing ethic of women will replace the greed and excessive need for dominance of patriarchal society, Rich believes that women must explore their collective consciousness and shared experience in order to transcend the fragmentation and isolation of their lives: "The fact of being separate/ enters your livelihood like a piece of furniture" ("When We Dead Awaken," 1971). In order to create community, each woman must confront her experience stripped of patriarchal myths: "You give up keeping track of anniversaries,/ you begin to write in your diaries/ more honestly than ever." Women need a new mythology, sustaining definitions of self that are not male-identified.

In order to learn how to reconstruct her life, Rich returns to the ancient history of women in an effort to recover their lost heritage:

> Even you, fellow-creature, sister,
> sitting across from me, dark with love,
> working like me to pick apart
> working with me to remake
> this trailing knitted thing, this cloth of darkness,
> this woman's garment, trying to save the skein.
> ("When We Dead Awaken," 1971)

This radical shift in perspective resulting from the decision to break free of male definitions of reality creates considerable psychic turmoil—the significance of love, sex, orgasm, marriage and children are questioned:

> *I do not know*
> *if sex is an illusion*
>
> *I do not know*
> *who I was when I did those things*
> *or who I said I was*
> *or whether I willed to feel*

9. For a discussion of the implications of feminism for a socialist community, see Herbert Marcuse, "Marxism and Feminism," *Women's Studies: An Interdisciplinary Journal*, Vol. 2, no. 3, 1974 [*Martin's note*].

> *what I had read about*
> *or who in fact was there with me*
> *or whether I knew, even then*
> *that there was doubt about these things*
> ("Dialogue," 1972)

In "Diving into the Wreck" (1972), the poet returns alone to the sea, the origin of life, to explore "the wreck" of civilization in an effort to determine what went wrong. She descends without a guide, with no set of rules, with no man-made divisions: "and there is no one/ to tell me when the ocean/ will begin." Submerged in primal beginnings, she must learn to "breathe differently," to "learn alone/ to turn my body without force/ in the deep element." In the depths of the sea, diving into the wreck, she completes the circle of life, resolving the tensions between mind and matter, male and female, subject and object:

> This is the place.
> And I am here, the mermaid whose dark hair
> streams black, the merman in his armored body.
> We circle silently
> about the wreck.
> We dive into the hold.
> I am she: I am he.

Confronting the waste and destruction of the wreck of which she is a part—"the drowned face," the hidden cargo "inside barrels/ half-wedged and left to rot," "the water-eaten log/ the fouled compass"— the poet accepts the wreck and learns what she can from it as a necessary prelude to beginning again.

In "The Phenomenology of Anger" (1972), Rich traces the evolution of "cleansing anger" exploring the connections between anger, depression and madness. Depression is the internalization of anger resulting in excessive rumination, loss of energy and purpose —"self-hatred, a monotone in the mind." Women commonly experience depression because they are conditioned not to express rage—it is unfeminine to be angry. Frequently, madness and suicide are extreme anger turned inward resulting in the death of the self.

Rich deplores the distortion of psychic energy through which the unchecked aggression of men results in murder and warfare, and the repressed rage of women results in serious depression, madness, and suicide. Instead of internalizing her anger, she permits herself the fantasy of destroying her enemy with his own weapons:

> White acetylene
> ripples from my body
> Effortlessly released

                            perfectly trained
                            on the true enemy

Now, she is the modern amazon doing battle with the oppressor
who guns "down the babies at My Lai," who destroys crops with
"some new sublimate."

Expressing anger helps the poet to define herself, enabling her to
separate her needs from the patriarch's satanic obsession with mas-
tery: "The prince of air and darkness/ computing body counts,/
masturbating/ in the factory/ of facts." She is able to say "I hate
you" to this man of no feeling, sustaining herself with the dream of
a community of people who are in touch with their emotions, who
have reverence for nature, for life: "I would have loved to live in
a world/ of women and men gaily/ in collusion with green leaves."
But this is a utopian vision in a world where machines hurtle us
through space, poison our air and water, anesthetizing us to our
bodies, to nature.

Anger persists as a dominant emotion in Part III of *Diving into
the Wreck* and is an index of the poet's desire to create a new world:
"For weeks now a rage/ has possessed my body, driving/ now out
upon men and women/ now inward upon myself ("Merced," 1972).
Railing against the "world masculinity made / unfit for women or
men," she decries the emotional aridity and moral numbness of pa-
triarchal culture. Rage, then, is an energizing force, an emotion
which provides an impetus for social change.

Rich begins to understand the potential power of women and
men's fear of this power:

            If I am flesh sunning on rock
            if I am brain burning in fluorescent light
            if I am dream like a wire with fire
            throbbing along it
            if I am death to man
            I have to know it
                            ("August," 1972)

Rejecting patriarchal territoriality which defines women and chil-
dren as possessions, she resolves to find her matrilineal antecedents:[1]

            His mind is too simple, I cannot go on
            sharing his nightmares.
            My own are becoming clearer, they open
            into prehistory
            which looks like a village lit with blood
            where all the fathers are crying: *My son is mine!*
                            ("August")

1. For a discussion of the possible ma-
triarchal origins of society see J. J.
Bachofen, *Myth, Religion and Mother
Right* (Princeton: Princeton University
Press, 1967); Robert Briffault, *The
Mothers* (1927; reissued, New York:
Johnson Reprints, 1969); Robert Graves,
The White Goddess (New York: Farrar,
Straus & Giroux, 1966); Eric Neumann,
The Great Mother (Princeton: Prince-
ton University Press, 1972) [*Martin's
note*].

In "From an Old House in America," Rich insists that the modern woman must make demands of the men who have for centuries prescribed the boundaries of women's lives. She asks the question all women must ultimately ask the men in their lives: "What will you undertake"—what personal and political changes are men willing to make to demonstrate good faith, to demonstrate a genuine desire to abolish patriarchy?

> Will you punish me for history
> he said
>
> What will you undertake
> she said
>
> do you believe in collective guilt
> he said
>
> let me look into your eyes
> she said

No "man-hater," the poet nevertheless refuses to blind herself to the reality of the conflict between women and men in sexist society which is sterile, "autistic" with no reverence for life—for the female principle:

> The irreducible, incomplete connection
> between the dead and living
>
> or between man and woman in this
> savagely fathered and unmothered world

Tenderness, nurturance, a willingess to care about life in its most basic aspects—about children, about plants and animals—is unimportant in patriarchal culture.

Rich reviews the history of American women "washed up on this continent/ shipped here to be fruitful," to give birth to sons who will continue to dominate and exploit women and the land. In contrast to the wandering, solitary American hero who is not attached to family or community, the American woman remains at home alone to care for her children: "When the men hit the hobo track/ I stay on with the children." The solitude of the American woman does not have its origin in pride or a sense of adventure, but in necessity, "Most of the time, in my sex, I was alone." However, the fact that women have endured this involuntary isolation is evidence of strength and power: "my power is brief and local/ but I know my power."

The patriarchal insistence on "Law," the substitution of abstract principles for careful, reverent observation of life, has its origin in the fear and defensive hatred of the female principle and of women who are more closely connected to life by the reality of blood and birth: "his mother-hatred driving him/ into exile from the earth." Rich observes that our society with its simplification of the complexity of natural and human life, reflects the reality of men who were driven by the zealous desire to build a "city on a hill," pillaging the earth in the name of God's commonwealth: "It was made over-simple all along/ the separation of powers/ the allotment of sufferings."

Pondering the chthonic mysteries, the poet laments the denial of the ancient power of women in patriarchal society which defines fertility and reproduction as a duty rather than as a source of power and strength. The control of women's bodies by men is based on a fear of women's sexuality and capacity to bear children; the very word "illegitimate"—out of law—reveals a fear of uncontrolled female eros that threatens to make chaos of patriarchal social order: "Such women are dangerous to the order of things." Law, then, protects male property rights, male territoriality.

Patriarchs fear the sexual power of women and this fear contaminates the love of men and women making tenderness difficult or impossible. Women are badly damaged by the failures of love resulting from the male need for mastery—each failure leaves a scar, sadness, bitterness and finally fury:

> If it was lust that defined us—
> their lust and fears of our deep places
>
> we have done our time
> as faceless torsos licked by fire

But "lust and fear" provide a "key" to teach women how to preserve their power and not to offer it as a palliative to fearful men.

Becoming a midwife to a new age and at the same time giving birth to herself, Rich rejects the "genital contests" of the patriarchs which make community impossible. She insists that women must avoid the hubris of competitiveness, the snare of individualism—the struggle of women to create a life-oriented society is a collective struggle: "Any woman's death diminishes me."

Rich returns to the ancient origins of the community of women in order to more fully comprehend her own experience as a modern woman; this poetic exploration of matriarchal community—of the female principle—has important political consequences. Her poetry provides an organizing pattern for an intricate and complex cluster of perceptions which comprise the reality of the modern woman. As a feminist poet, Rich contributes her radical subjectivity to political process: that is, by analyzing and articulating her experience as a woman in patriarchal culture, by making private perceptions public, she establishes a coherent point of view, a feminist identity and poetic vision which becomes part of the composite reality of a community. Her poetry, then, like all good poetry changes the way we perceive and experience the world.

NANCY MILFORD

This Woman's Movement †

Believe me when I tell you that there have been so few women who wrote and who continued to write and did not fall silent. Who were they and in what context of time did they live and write? Where, for instance, were the women who married in their youth and bore children and continued to write? Do you remember Tillie Olsen's first published story, and was it an accident that it begins: "I stand here ironing, and what you asked me moves tormented back and forth with the iron"?

There were some of course who chose men, or who were chosen by them, men who educated them perhaps, or who led them into their rooms not for lovemaking or childbearing alone, but led them there that they might gain the confidence and the time to write undisturbed. Colette, Virginia Woolf, Lillian Hellman, and even Simone de Beauvoir and Mary McCarthy come to mind. But were the doors to those rooms sealed in special ways, I wonder, sealed from the full province of a woman's experience, or from the experience she might rightfully select for herself? And even if they were not, were there not conditions to be met, hazardous to either the woman herself or to the man who had provided her with that room, that sealed door, that lack of disturbance?

Think of the women who have written: the unmarried, the married and childless, the very few with a single child and that one observed as if it were a rock to be stubbed against. Jane Austen, the Brontës, Christina Rossetti, Elizabeth Barrett Browning, Emily Dickinson, George Eliot, Edith Wharton, Willa Cather, Dorothy Richardson, Katharine Mansfield, Gertrude Stein, Marianne Moore, Edna St. Vincent Millay, H. D., Elinor Wylie, Anaïs Nin, and Sylvia Plath. Has it been truly different in our own generation?

Still, lists don't mean much. It is only that there have been so few women who wrote well. And why is it that among them there are certain limits of range—or at the least recognizable types whose critical reputations seem to me to exceed either their abilities or their voices? In the past we have had an abundance of chaste women, reclusive and withdrawn—perhaps for the sake of their own sur-

† Copyright © 1975 by Nancy Milford.

vival as writers. Adrienne Rich wrote about the best of them,
Emily Dickinson:

> and in your half-cracked way you chose
> silence for entertainment,
> chose to have it out at last
> on your own premises.

And the crazy ladies, our maimed heroines; those suicidal, mad or
martyred women whose flashing energy is revealed in poems that
prophesy and then fulfill their need for self-destruction. (I would
not like to be caught saying that poets cannot be chaste or self-
destructive and earn our respect as writers: both Dickinson and
Sylvia Plath have that respect; and I am not, I think, asking for
healthy poems written by women willing to reproduce, but I am
asking what it may mean about us that these poets survive with
high esteem in our own time and why it is that they and not others
have become our heroines?)

Where is that woman in the prime of her life, telling us what
she sees and feels and dreams of? She who has found her own voice
and permits us to witness not only the finding as an act in itself—
within the poems—but gives up to us what she has found? For
"We're living through a time / that needs to be lived through us."
Are we not?

I

I believe that the best poetry is marked by the passionate and
personal voice of the poet expressed in the strong rhythms of our
speech. For it seems to me that all good writing comes out of our
personal life, "out of its tragedy," as Yeats once said of his own
work, "whatever it be, remorse, lost love or mere loneliness. . . ."
What we need of criticism is a voice to discern and apprehend the
poet's achievement in order to break down the barrier between the
work and the reader of the work, between the poetic utterance and
the private hearing.

I wrote my first piece on Adrienne Rich when I was twenty and
I wrote it as if I had discovered her. I was taking a course in the
writing of poetry and as our final assignment the poet who was
teaching the course, and with whom I was half in love, asked us to
pick any poet under forty who we thought would last. I had read
Rich at first because I knew she had been at Radcliffe at the same
time he was at Harvard. But so much for mixed motives; when most
of my classmates selected Robert Lowell, I chose Adrienne Rich
because I had found in her work poems to like, poems that although

never confessional or merely autobiographical were nevertheless marked by what she once said Anne Bradstreet's best work possessed, "life-giving strokes of personal facts."

This was in 1959, after her first two books had been published, and for several years she had published no book. I worried over the silence and wondered what was causing it. Had she lost her voice? She and I were a decade apart in age and I knew nothing much about being the sort of woman she was: a woman who had experienced a fine success with her first book, which was published in the Yale Younger Poet series, and who had been put on contract by *The New Yorker;* a woman who had married and had young children. And I knew nothing at all about the uncertainty and fear that may accompany success. It had never occurred to me that I might belong to generations of women, was one among them in fact, and I suppose if I had been asked I would have said that I was without a shared past. It was for me all Future and Promise and Destiny and Hard Work.

Now my hunch is that the worlds we inhabit are kindred and connecting, and that I hear in her voice the nerve and swing my own lacks. Maybe that's the use of poetry and of art: not that it guides us, but that it gives us a reach and a purchase we do not have without the poems; that it aids us to see and to feel what we have not seen or felt clearly before; and even that in this seeing and feeling we open out. I think I can claim of Adrienne Rich's poetry that although it exists in and of itself, apprehending it we are in some fashion changed, renewed maybe, made fresh.

II

Adrienne Rich has published seven books of poetry. The first, *A Change of World,* was published in 1951, when she was twenty-one, and the last, *Diving into the Wreck,* in 1973.[1] It is within these volumes that we may find the author's self, in them that the growth of that self may properly be apprehended; and it is this growth taking its shape in particular poems that I am after. For I believe that we may learn from her movement not only where she has been, and the manner of her travels to where she is now, but also something about the increasingly political thrust of her work. By political I mean those acts of conduct within her own time, that governance of her self among other selves, through which she tries to come to terms with her sex in this time. Which is after all our own.

1. This essay was written in the summer of 1974, before the publication of *Poems: Selected and New.*

III

Form is the ultimate gift that love can offer—
The vital union of necessity
With all that we desire, all that we suffer.

A too-compassionate art is half an art.
Only such proud restraining purity
Restores the else-betrayed, too-human heart.
("At a Bach Concert," *A Change of World*)

She was in her first book of poems what Auden suggested in his introduction to it: modest. Her poems were often derivative, but they made full admission of their antecedents. She was, then, a young woman of a certain education; her voice was quiet but clear enough to be heard plainly, and she did not fib. Auden said that these qualities were enough to distinguish a first volume: "Radical changes and significant novelty in artistic style can only occur when there has been a radical change in human sensibility to require them. The spectacular events of the present time must not blind us to the fact that we are living not at the beginning but in the middle of an historical epoch. . . ." Her concerns were with form and with restraint in that a violation of restraint spelt excess, and excess in art as in life was bad-mannered, possibly destructive and essentially (given our middle epoch) uncalled for. But even in this first volume there were poems to like. "Storm Warnings" [2] was one. The only problem with the book was that her own voice was thin, it was not rich enough.

IV

Between her second book, *The Diamond Cutters,* in 1955 and her third, *Snapshots of a Daughter-in-Law,* in 1963, there were eight years of silence. Those were years in which poems were written (we can tell by the dates she has given them in *Snapshots*), but in which no book took shape. They were also the years of early marriage, the birthing and raising of three sons to school age.

Snapshots was a departure, not only because within it are a remarkable group of poems—the title poem as well as "Merely to Know," "Double Monologue," and "Readings of History"—but also because Rich who had always had a sense of the past ("Storm Warnings" shows her in apprehension before it) was now set to examine it closely, to find what it held in especial for her; and to ask herself also whether even that reading was done "to shut out

2. In the original essay the text of "Storm Warnings" was quoted here. It appears in this book on p. 1.

the tick-tock of self." I don't think anybody else who was writing then was asking these questions in this way and with this degree of scrutiny. The past held plenty, and as she explored it the tidiness and the modesty fell away. In the poem "From Morning-Glory to Petersburg," dated 1954, she put it this way:

I can recall when knowledge still was pure,
    not contradictory, pleasurable
    as cutting out a paper doll.
You opened up a book and there it was:
    everything just as promised. . . .
    Facts could be kept separate
    by a convention; . . .
    Now knowledge finds me out;
    in all its risible untidiness
    it traces me to each address,
dragging in things I never thought about.
    I don't invite what facts can be
    held at arm's length; a family
of jeering irresponsibles always
    come along gypsy-style
    and there you have them all
forever on your hands. It never pays.
    ("From Morning-Glory to Petersburg," *Snapshots*)

But four years later, in the poem "Snapshots of a Daughter-in-Law," written between 1958 and 1960, she decided to write about the "situation of some women of our time," and in so doing she confronted full face what the history of these women suggested—the odds against any woman doing, making anything difficult of her own, for her own sake, for her own use. The poem breaks into ten sections, moving from the observation of an older woman (and mother) "once a belle in Shreveport,"

Your mind now, moldering like wedding-cake,
heavy with useless experience, rich
with suspicion, rumor, fantasy,
crumbling to pieces under the knife-edge
of mere fact. In the prime of your life.

to a "thinking woman sleep[ing] with monsters"; past Emily Dickinson, "Reading while waiting/ for the iron to heat,/ writing, *My Life had stood—a Loaded Gun*"; to that woman who even in song finds "neither words nor music are her own":

. . . Pinned down
by love, for you the only natural action,
are you edged more keen
to prise the secrets of the vault? has Nature shown

> her household books to you, daughter-in-law,
> that her sons never saw?

In the final sections of the poem, recognizing those odds she fights against them. But the risk taken, she says, of casting "too bold a shadow" or of smashing "the mould straight off" leads women into loneliness, or worse "solitary confinement."

>   Well,
> she's long about her coming, who must be
> more merciless to herself than history.
> Her mind full to the wind, I see her plunge
> breasted and glancing through the currents,
> taking the light upon her
> at least as beautiful as any boy
> or helicopter,
>   poised, still coming,
> her fine blades making the air wince
> but her cargo
> no promise then:
> delivered
> palpable
> ours.

But this cargo is in a constant state of deliverance and the poet will play it out, shaping, making in effect what cargo she is capable of.

And yet what is a snapshot? A quick-take, a candid perhaps; a picture that does not suggest the formality of the artist making a portrait, but SNAP/SHOT—that vision taken on the run of people and of things caught unaware, frozen in time, which is always time past. The intellectual momentum of this book, while relentless, is very like the snapshot. Rich continues to be caught either within the range of the camera held in someone else's hand, or in her own, and the camera as well as the images of the camera become a device for recording and for keeping distance—not truly for seeing.

In "Readings of History," written in the year "Snapshots" was completed, she asks whether even the act of apprehending the past (literally, *reading* about it) is not an effort to achieve distance. In the first part of the poem, called "The Evil Eye," she again uses photographic equipment as the vehicle through which the poet perceives. But if the stereopticon into which she gazes provides contact with the past, it shows the past distorted and dead, and she is left terrified by the vision.

> Today, a fresh clean morning.
> Your camera stabs me unawares,
> right in my mortal part.

> A womb of celluloid already
> contains my dotage and my total absence.

She seems to be asking questions of the past that suggest shadow questions in the present: What happened? becomes *what is happening?* Who were we?/ *Who am I now?*

> Can history show us nothing
> but pieces of ourselves, detached,
> set to a kind of poetry,
> a kind of music, even?
>
> . . . .
>
> Is it in hopes
> to find or lose myself
> that I
> fill up my table now
> with Michelet and Motley?
> To "know how it was"
> or to forget how it is—
> what else?

And in another poem from this collection, "Double Monologue," she moves from stating her needs clearly ("I have wanted one thing: to know/ simply as I know my name/ at any given moment, where I stand") to asking what is the good of having such self-knowledge, when she knows that the self slips and changes in its growth and is not therefore as exact as any scrutiny of it suggests:

> Don't think I think
> facts serve better than ignorant love.
> Both serve, and still
> our need mocks our gear.

v

In *Necessities of Life* Rich held the ground she had taken. But she seemed to be collecting herself—collecting as a horse is collected by the rider in order to bring him all eagerness and urgency to the barrier that he may not shy from it, but clear it. So in *Necessities of Life* she was writing with high care, with a certain held-in energy which gave some of the poems their special edge. From the title poem:

> whole biographies swam up and
> swallowed me like Jonah.
>
> Jonah! I was Wittgenstein,
> Mary Wollstonecraft, the soul

> of Louis Jouvet, dead
> in a blown-up phototograph.
>
> Till, wolfed almost to shreds,
> I learned to make myself
>
> unappetizing. . . .
>
> I used myself, let nothing use me.
>
> . . . .
>
> What life was there, was mine.
>
> now and again to lay
> one hand on a warm brick
>
> and touch the sun's ghost
> with economical joy,
>
> now and again to name
> over the bare necessities.
>
> So much for those days.

The best poems, "Like This Together," "Two Songs," "Night-Pieces: For a Child," and "Not Like That" were filled by recapitulation, attempts to define precisely where she was then, and by notes of loss.

> But you and I—
> swaddled in a dumb dark
> old as sickheartedness,
> modern as pure annihilation—
>
> we drift in ignorance.
> If I could hear you now
> mutter some gentle animal sound!
> If milk flowed from my breast again. . . .
> ("Night-Pieces: For a Child")

Leaflets, published three years later, in 1969, was the beginning of that long clear leap forward. In it she affirmed her craft, "Only where there is language is there world," and began the far more difficult affirmation of herself as a woman (although in most of these poems it was still as a woman speaking to a man). She asserted that language could achieve change, that naming was another form of making real.

> I wanted to choose words that even you
> would have to be changed by
>
> Take the word
> of my pulse, loving and ordinary
> Send out your signals, hoist

> your dark scribbled flags
> but take
> my hand
>
> All wars are useless to the dead
> ("Implosions")

But perhaps the real achievement in these poems was in the kind
of poet she had risked becoming; living in a time of break-up, op-
pression and violence, she took these things for her own ground and
she was partisan. She chose to turn from being the precise and
somewhat remote observer of her earlier work; she threw the weight
of her voice and of her poetic skill into passionate resistance. I do
not mean to say that she became imprecise, but rather that her
poetry accommodated her turning—her lines became less regular
and the rhythms that supported them were increasingly broken, even
her voice grew more colloquial.

> It's true   there are moments
> closer and closer together
> when words stick   in my throat
>   *the art of love*
>   *the art of words*
> I get your message Gabriel
> just   will you stay looking
> straight at me
> awhile longer
>
>   ("Gabriel")

Maybe the toll of such willingness to risk and to see was an inevi-
table loneliness. For even in a gentle poem like "In The Evening"
her sense of being separate grows sharp and cries out in the final
stanza with its internal sounds of long vowels stretched like moans.[3]
In "Nightbreak" the structure of the poem supported its content;
it was as jagged as anger is.

> Something broken   Something
> I need   By someone
> I love   Next year
> will I remember what
> This anger   unreal
>   yet
> has to be gone through

It was in these poems written in 1968, and especially in "Leaflets"
and in her "Ghazals: Homage to Ghalib" written during the summer
of 1968, that she formed her moral voice. I call it moral because
she was saying "This is how life must be lived."

---

3. See pp. 36–37, above, for "In the Evening." (In the original essay the text was
quoted at this point.)

life without caution
the only worth living
love for a man
love for a woman
love for the facts
protectless

that self-defense be not
the arm's first motion

memory not only
cards of identity

that I can live half a year
as I have never lived up to this time—

. . . .

We're fighting for a slash of recognition,
a piercing to the pierced heart.
Tell me what you are going through—

. . . .

   I want to hand you this
leaflet streaming with rain or tears
   but the words coming clear
something you might find crushed into your hands
   after passing a barricade
and stuff in your raincoat pocket.
   I want this to reach you
who once told me that poetry is nothing sacred
   —no more sacred that is
than other things in your life—
   to answer yes, if life is uncorrupted
no better poetry is wanted.

. . . .

   What else does it come down to
but handing on scraps of paper . . .
because the imagination crouches in them.
("Leaflets")

But this moral voice was achieved at some cost to the poetry; often
the lines were long and marked by statement, by judgments. There
was a rush and urgency in them as they moved into those zones
which are usually set aside for prose. They were, in other words,
poems of commitment, and as such they ran the risk of being pro-
saic. Some of them were in direct address to the reader:

Don't look for me in the room I have left;
the photograph shows just a white rocking-chair, still rocking.
("Ghazals: Homage to Ghalib, 7/13/68")

Did you think I was talking about my life?
I was trying to drive a tradition up against the wall.
             ("Ghazals: Homage to Ghalib, 7/14/68:ii")

Still, filled as they were with the moral outrage of the late sixties, there was very little of its rhetoric, and the best of the "Ghazals" were bound to the rest of her work by shared themes, images and anger:

7/24/68: i

The sapling springs, the milkweed blooms: obsolete Nature.
In the woods I have a vision of asphalt, blindly lingering.

I hardly know the names of the weeds I love.
I have forgotten the names of so many flowers.

I can't live at the hem of that tradition—
will I last to try the beginning of the next?

Killing is different now: no fingers round the throat.
No one feels the wetness of the blood on his hands.

When we fuck, there too are we remoter
than the fucking bodies of lovers used to be?

How many men have touched me with their eyes
More hotly than they later touched me with their lips.

VI

I want a heroine. A woman who will stand her ground, knowing at what cost she stands, spending herself in that stance, damaged and perhaps inevitably self-damaging, because to open fresh territory comes hard and is against the grain of any age. But she who touches and wrests from her own unconscious its secret and lavish fruits and brings them to us ripe is heroic. And we have great need of her.

What we see, we see
and seeing is changing.

·   ·   ·   ·   ·   ·   ·   ·   ·   ·   ·   ·   ·   ·

I am bombarded yet   I stand
I have been standing all my life in the
direct path of a battery of signals
the most accurately transmitted most
untranslatable language in the universe
I am a galactic cloud so deep   so invo-
luted that a light wave could take 15
years to travel through me   And has
taken   I am an instrument in the shape

> of a woman trying to translate pulsations
> into images   for the relief of the body
> and the reconstruction of the mind.
> > ("Planetarium," *The Will to Change*)

In these poems Adrienne Rich is working out the destiny of her paradoxical identities: American woman and American poet. I do not know much about her life and I have only her poems in which to locate her; but when I say American woman is that enough? An American woman living through that time of radical change in human sensibility that Auden said had not come. But that was a quarter of a century ago and Auden is dead.

> knowledge of the oppressor
> this is the oppressor's language
>
> Yet I need it to talk to you

What could have prepared her for the violence and the poverty and the oppression she has been witness to and that has inescapably marred her own life? Yet confronting it she has made a grammar to hold what she has found.

> *People suffer highly in poverty and it takes dignity and intelligence to overcome this suffering. Some of the suffering are: a child did not had dinner last night: a child steal because he did not have money to buy it: to hear a mother say she do not have money to buy food for her children and to see a child without cloth it will make tears in your eyes.*

> (the fracture of order
> the repair of speech
> to overcome this suffering)
> ("The Burning of Paper Instead of Children," *The Will to Change*)

In "Shooting Script," the series of poems that ends *The Will to Change,* she focuses on fragments of her own past; moving and recording with grave eloquence she seems to be saying goodbye to that sense of her self that "was looking for a way out of a lifetime's consolations," that was "Entering the poem as a method of leaving the room."

We are driven to odd attempts; once it would not have occurred to me to put out in a boat, not on a night like this.

Still it was an instrument, and I had pledged myself to try any instrument that came my way. Never to refuse one from conviction of incompetence.

A long time I was simply learning to handle the skiff; I had no special training and my own training was against me.

I had always heard that darkness and water were a threat.

In spite of this, darkness and water helped me to arrive here.

I watched the lights on the shore I had left for a long time; each one, it seemed to me, was a light I might have lit, in the old days.

("Shooting Script," II, 13)

VII

Darkness and water. In *Diving into the Wreck* she enters more deeply than ever before into female fantasy; and these are primal waters, life-giving and secretive in the special sense of not being wholly revealed. The female element. A diver may dive to plunder or to explore.

> First having read the book of myths,
> and loaded the camera,
> and checked the edge of the knife-blade,
> I put on
> the body-armor of black rubber
> the absurd flippers
> the grave and awkward mask.

Alone and crippled by her equipment, she is descending, she is "having to do this," "and there is no one / to tell me when the ocean / will begin." And even though the mask of the diver is powerful the point of the dive is not the exercise of power in self-defense.

> the sea is not a question of power
> I have to learn alone
> to turn my body without force
> in the deep element

She came "to explore the wreck." And what is the wreckage; is it of marriage, or of sex, or of the selfhood within each? Is it the female body, her own?

> This is the place.
> And I am here, the mermaid whose dark hair
> streams black, the merman in his armored body
> We circle silently
> about the wreck
> we dive into the hold.
> I am she: I am he

Moving in deeply private images, circling darkly and richly into the very sources of her poetry, she is, as she says,[4] "coming-home to . . . sex, sexuality, sexual wounds, sexual identity, sexual politics":

> we are the half-destroyed instruments
> that once held to a course

4. In a statement by the poet on the dust-jacket of *Diving into the Wreck*.

the water-eaten log
the fouled compass

We are, I am, you are
by cowardice or courage
the one who find our way
back to this scene
carrying a knife, a camera
a book of myths
in which
our names do not appear.

Dreaming of the person within the poem: she walking toward me, naked, swaying, bending down, her dark long hair falling forward of its own weight like heavy cloth shielding my face and her own, her full breasts brushing my cheek, moving toward my mouth. The dream is the invention of the dreamer, and the content of the dream moves in symbols of sustenance and of comfort. The hands of that diving woman become our own hands, reaching out, touching, holding; not in sex but in deliverance. That is the potency of her poetry: it infuses dreams, it makes possible connections between people in the face of what seems to be irrevocable separateness, it forges an alliance between the poet and the reader. The power of her woman's voice crying out, *I am*: surviving, sustaining, continuing, and making whole

we move together like underwater plants

Over and over, starting to wake
I dive back to discover you
still whispering, *touch me,* we go on
streaming through the slow
citylight forest ocean
stirring our body hair

But this is the saying of a dream
on waking
I wish there were somewhere
actual we could stand
handing the power-glasses back and forth
looking at the earth, the wildwood
where the split began
                    ("Waking in the Dark")

Chronology

<table>
<tr><td>1929</td><td>Born in Baltimore, Maryland, May 16. Began writing poetry as a child under the encouragement and supervision of her father, Dr. Arnold Rich, from whose "very Victorian, pre-Raphaelite" library, Rich later recalled, she read Tennyson, Keats, Arnold, Blake, Rossetti, Swinburne, Carlyle, and Pater.</td></tr>
<tr><td>1951</td><td>A.B., Radcliffe College. Phi Beta Kappa. A Change of World chosen by W. H. Auden for the Yale Younger Poets Award and published.</td></tr>
<tr><td>1952–53</td><td>Guggenheim Fellowship; travel in Europe and England.</td></tr>
<tr><td>1953</td><td>Marriage to Alfred H. Conrad, an economist who taught at Harvard. Residence in Cambridge, Massachusetts, 1953–66.</td></tr>
<tr><td>1955</td><td>Birth of David Conrad. Publication of The Diamond Cutters and Other Poems, which won the Ridgely Torrence Memorial Award of the Poetry Society of America.</td></tr>
<tr><td>1957</td><td>Birth of Paul Conrad.</td></tr>
<tr><td>1959</td><td>Birth of Jacob Conrad.</td></tr>
<tr><td>1960</td><td>National Institute of Arts and Letters Award for poetry. Phi Beta Kappa poet at William and Mary College.</td></tr>
<tr><td>1961–62</td><td>Guggenheim Fellowship; residence with family in the Netherlands.</td></tr>
<tr><td>1962</td><td>Bollingen Foundation grant for translation of Dutch poetry.</td></tr>
<tr><td>1962–63</td><td>Amy Lowell Travelling Fellowship.</td></tr>
<tr><td>1963</td><td>Snapshots of a Daughter-in-Law published. Bess Hokin Prize of Poetry magazine.</td></tr>
<tr><td>1965</td><td>Phi Beta Kappa poet at Swarthmore College.</td></tr>
<tr><td>1966</td><td>Necessities of Life published, nominated for the National Book Award. Phi Beta Kappa poet at Harvard College. Move to New York City, where Alfred Conrad taught at City College of New York. Residence there from 1966 on. Increasingly active politically in protests against the Indochina war.</td></tr>
<tr><td>1966–68</td><td>Lecturer at Swarthmore College.</td></tr>
<tr><td>1967–69</td><td>Adjunct Professor of Writing in the Graduate School of the Arts, Columbia University.</td></tr>
<tr><td>1967</td><td>Selected Poems published in Britain. Litt.D., Wheaton College.</td></tr>
</table>

1968 Eunice Tietjens Memorial Prize of *Poetry* magazine. Began teaching in the SEEK and Open Admissions Programs at City College of New York.

1969 *Leaflets* published.

1970 Death of Alfred Conrad.

1971 *The Will to Change* published. Shelley Memorial Award of the Poetry Society of America. Increasingly identifies with the women's movement as a radical feminist.

1972–73 Fanny Hurst Visiting Professor of Creative Literature at Brandeis University.

1973 *Diving into the Wreck* published.

1973–74 Ingram Merrill Foundation research grant; began work on a book on the history and myths of motherhood.

1974 National Book Award for *Diving into the Wreck*. Rich rejected the award as an individual, but accepted it, in a statement written with Audre Lord and Alice Walker, two other nominees, in the name of all women:

> "We . . . together accept this award in the name of all the women whose voices have gone and still go unheard in a patriarchal world, and in the name of those who, like us, have been tolerated as token women in this culture, often at great cost and in great pain. . . . We symbolically join here in refusing the terms of patriarchal competition and declaring that we will share this prize among us, to be used as best we can for women. . . . We dedicate this occasion to the struggle for self-determination of all women, of every color, identification or derived class . . . the women who will understand what we are doing here and those who will not understand yet; the silent women whose voices have been denied us, the articulate women who have given us strength to do our work."

Professor of English, City College of New York.

1975 *Poems: Selected and New* published.

Bibliography

I. VOLUMES OF POEMS

A Change of World. New Haven: Yale University Press, 1951.
The Diamond Cutters and Other Poems. New York: Harper, 1955.
Snapshots of a Daughter-in-Law. New York: Harper & Row, 1963; re-
issued, New York: W. W. Norton, 1967; London: Chatto & Windus,
1970.
Necessities of Life. New York: W. W. Norton, 1966.
Selected Poems. London: Chatto & Windus, 1967.
Leaflets. New York: W. W. Norton, 1969; London: Chatto & Windus,
1972.
The Will to Change. New York: W. W. Norton, 1971; London: Chatto
& Windus, 1973.
Diving into the Wreck. New York: W. W. Norton, 1973.
Poems: Selected and New. New York: W. W. Norton, 1975.

II. ESSAYS AND REVIEWS

"Review of *The Lordly Hudson* by Paul Goodman." *The New York Re-
view of Books* (1st issue, undated, 1963), p. 27.
"Mr. Bones, He Lives: Review of *77 Dream Songs* by John Berryman."
The Nation, CXCVIII, 22 (May 25, 1964), 538, 540.
"Beyond the Heirlooms of Tradition: Review of *Found Objects* by Louis
Zukofsky." *Poetry,* CV, 2 (November, 1964), 128–129.
"Reflections on Lawrence: Review of *The Complete Poems of D. H.
Lawrence.*" *Poetry,* CVI, 3 (June, 1965), 218–225.
"On Karl Shapiro's *The Bourgeois Poet.*" In *The Contemporary Poet as
Artist and Critic,* ed. Anthony Ostroff. Boston: Little, Brown, 1964;
pp. 192–194.
"Foreword: Anne Bradstreet and Her Poetry." In *The Works of Anne
Bradstreet,* ed. Jeannine Hensley. Cambridge, Mass.: Harvard Uni-
versity Press, 1967; pp. ix–xx.
"Living with Henry: Review of *His Toy, His Dream, His Rest* by John
Berryman." *The Harvard Advocate* (John Berryman Issue), CIII,
1 (Spring, 1969), 10–11.
"For Randall Jarrell." In *Randall Jarrell 1914–1965,* ed. Robert Lowell,
Peter Taylor, and Robert Penn Warren. New York: Farrar, Straus
& Giroux, 1967; pp. 182–183.
"Review of *Pilgrims* by Jean Valentine." *Chicago Review,* XXII, 1 (Au-
tumn, 1970), 128–130.
"A Tool or a Weapon: Review of *For You* and *The Clay Hill Anthology*
by Hayden Carruth." *The Nation,* CCXIII, 13 (October 25, 1971),
408–410.

"Introduction to 'Poems from Prison' by Luis Talamantez." *Liberation,* XVI, 16 (November, 1971), 10.

"When We Dead Awaken: Writing as Re-Vision." *College English,* XXXIV, 1 (October, 1972), 18–25.

"Poetry, Personality, and Wholeness: A Response to Galway Kinnell." *Field: Contemporary Poetry and Poetics,* 7 (Fall, 1972), 11–18.

"Review of *Welcome Eumenides* by Eleanor Ross Taylor." *The New York Times Book Review,* July 2, 1972, p. 3.

"The Anti-Feminist Woman: Review Essay on *The New Chastity and Other Arguments Against Women's Liberation* by Midge Decter." *The New York Review of Books,* XIX, 9 (November 30, 1972), 34–40.

"Voices in the Wilderness: Review of *Monster* by Robin Morgan." *The Washington Post Book World,* December 31, 1972, p. 3.

"Review of *Women and Madness* by Phyllis Chesler." *The New York Times Book Review,* December 31, 1972, pp. 1, 20–21.

"Review of *The Women Poets in English: An Anthology* edited by Ann Stanford." *The New York Times Book Review,* April 15, 1973, p. 6.

"Teaching Language in Open Admissions: A Look at the Context." *The Uses of Literature,* ed. Monroe Engel (Harvard English Studies, 4). Cambridge, Mass.: Harvard University Press, 1973; pp. 257–273.

"Jane Eyre: The Temptations of a Motherless Woman." *Ms.,* II, 4 (October, 1973), 68–72, 98, 106–107.

"The Sisterhood of Man: Review of *Beyond God the Father: Toward a Philosophy of Women's Liberation* by Mary Daly." *The Washington Post Book World,* November 11, 1973, pp. 2–3.

"Caryatid: A Column." *The American Poetry Review,* II, 1 (January/February, 1973); II, 3 (May/June, 1973); II, 5 (September/October, 1973).

"Toward A Woman-Centered University," in a forthcoming volume on women and higher education edited by Florence Howe, to be published in 1975 by the Carnegie Commission on the Future of Higher Education.

III. INTERVIEWS

Robert Shaw and John Plotz. "An Interview with Adrienne Rich." *The Island,* I, 3 (May, 1966), 2–8.

David Kalstone. "Talking with Adrienne Rich." *The Saturday Review: The Arts,* IV, 17 (April 22, 1972), 56–59.

Stanley Plumly, Wayne Dodd, and Walter Tevis. "Talking with Adrienne Rich." *The Ohio Review,* XIII, 1 (1971), 29–46.

IV. RECORDINGS

Adrienne Rich Reading At Stanford. The Stanford Program for Recordings in Sound, 1973. Introduction by Barbara Charlesworth Gelpi.

Jacket notes by Albert Gelpi. Recorded at a reading in January, 1973, with the poet reading: "Burning Oneself In," "Didactic Poem," "In the Evening," "I Dream I'm the Death of Orpheus," "Unwritten Novel," "The Fourth Month of the Landscape Architect," "Waking in the Dark," "Incipience," "The Stranger," "Merced," "A Primary Ground," "Translations," "The Phenomenology of Anger," "Diving into the Wreck."

Contributors

W. H. AUDEN (1907–1973) was judge for the Yale Younger Poets Award for many years, as he was when he made the award to Adrienne Rich in 1951. His volumes of poetry include: *Collected Longer Poems, Collected Shorter Poems, City Without Walls,* and *Epistle to a Godson.* His books of criticism include *The Dyer's Hand* and *Secondary Worlds.*

ROBERT BOYERS teaches at Skidmore College. He has co-edited *R. D. Laing and Anti-Psychiatry* and *Robert Lowell: A Portrait of the Artist in His Time,* writes on psychology and literature, and is editor-in-chief of *Salmagundi.*

ALBERT GELPI teaches at Stanford University. He is the author of *Emily Dickinson: The Mind of the Poet* and *The Tenth Muse: The Psyche of the American Poet,* and is editor of *The Poet in America 1650 to the Present.*

BARBARA CHARLESWORTH GELPI teaches at Stanford University. She has written *Dark Passages: The Decadent Consciousness in Victorian Literature* and has published essays on nineteenth-century British literature and on Jungian psychology. She is working on a study of the image of the androgyne in nineteenth-century social thought.

RANDALL JARRELL (1914–1965) has a *Complete Poems,* and his criticism includes *Poetry and the Age, Sad Heart at the Supermarket,* and *Third Book of Criticism.*

ERICA JONG teaches at City College of the City University of New York and is a poet (*Half-Lives* and *Fruits and Vegetables*) and novelist (*Fear of Flying*).

WENDY MARTIN teaches at Queens College of the City University of New York. She founded and edits *Women's Studies: An Interdisciplinary Journal,* and edited *The American Sisterhood: Writings of the Feminist Movement from Colonial Times to the Present.* In addition to essays on American women writers, she has also published essays on the early American novel. She is currently writing a book on American women writers.

NANCY MILFORD has written *Zelda,* the biography of Zelda Fitzgerald, and is at work on a full-scale biography of Edna St. Vincent Millay.

HELEN VENDLER teaches at Boston University. She is the author of *Yeats' Vision and the Later Plays; On Extended Wings: Wallace Stevens' Longer Poems;* and many essays on modern poets.

Index of Poems

Poems are listed by title and first line. Entries under title also indicate the pages on which the poem is discussed in the prose selections in this volume. Also listed are poems mentioned in the prose but not included in the present selection.

211

NORTON CRITICAL EDITIONS